*Serge A
Simple Project*

# Serge A Simple Project

Tammy Young
& Naomi Baker

Chilton Book Company
Radnor, Pennsylvania

Copyright © 1994 by Tammy Young and Naomi Baker

All Rights Reserved

Published in Radnor, Pennsylvania 19089, by Chilton Book Company

Designed by Rosalyn Carson

Illustrated by Chris Hansen

Manufactured in the United States of America

A CIP record for this book is available from the Library of Congress
ISBN 0-8019-8393-2

1 2 3 4 5 6 7 8 9 0   3 2 1 0 9 8 7 6 5 4

# Other Books Available From Chilton

# Other Books Available From Chilton (continued)

## KNOW YOUR SEWING MACHINE SERIES, BY JACKIE DODSON

**Know Your Bernina,** second edition

**Know Your Brother,** with Jane Warnick

**Know Your Elna,** with Carol Ahles

**Know Your New Home,** with Judi Cull and Vicki Lyn Hastings

**Know Your Pfaff,** with Audrey Griese

**Know Your Sewing Machine**

**Know Your Singer**

**Know Your Viking,** with Jan Saunders

**Know Your White,** with Jan Saunders

## KNOW YOUR SERGER SERIES, BY TAMMY YOUNG AND NAOMI BAKER

**Know Your baby lock**

**Know Your Pfaff Hobbylock**

**Know Your Serger**

**Know Your White Superlock**

## STAR WEAR SERIES

**Embellishments,** by Linda Fry Kenzie

**Make It Your Own,** by Lori Bottom and Ronda Chaney

**Sweatshirts with Style,** by Mary Mulari

## TEACH YOURSELF TO SEW BETTER SERIES, BY JAN SAUNDERS

**A Step-by Step Guide to Your Bernina**

**A Step-by Step Guide to Your New Home**

**A Step-by Step Guide to Your Sewing Machine**

**A Step-by Step Guide to Your Viking**

# Contents

# Foreword

BY NANCY ZIEMAN

*L*et's face it—many of us who are sewing enthusiasts would rather sew or serge than shop, unless it's shopping in a fabric store. Just this weekend I was looking for a gift and becoming more anxious by the minute. (I get more nervous when shopping than taping TV shows!) Finally, I spotted the perfect vest for my sister and picked up the price tag. It was more than slightly overpriced, but I thought, "It's for my sister!" I was just ready to make the purchase when I checked the quality. Yikes, what terrible workmanship—I knew I could make that vest, knew it will stay together! Assured that it wasn't a good day to shop, I went home to the retreat of my sewing room.

That evening I read the final draft of this book, *Serge A Simple Project*. In the comfort of my home, I found that my friends Naomi and Tammy had once again streamlined serging, plus given project after project to serge and sew. It was so relaxing thinking about what I could make with just a few sewing steps and nominal fabrics and supplies. I found myself mentally planning a gift list, not analyzing a book. But then I came to page 34—a Tapestry Vest. It looked just like the one I had almost bought. Why had I wasted time shopping? In a little over two pages of instructions, Naomi and Tammy had given me all I needed to know.

That's what *Serge A Simple Project* is all about: **it's all you need to know about 48 projects.** Naomi and Tammy did the shopping, tested the techniques, streamlined the process, and wrote clear instructions. What more could you want?

The next time I need a gift, my first stop will be at my bookshelf with *Serge A Simple Project*. Whew! I like this kind of shopping.

# Acknowledgments

Every sewing enthusiast has someone she can point to who inspired her to sew, and we would like to acknowledge and thank those who influenced us:

Naomi's late grandmother, Helena Loseke, taught her as a child to sew on a treadle sewing machine. Her mother, Marcella Loseke, a superb seamstress, motivated her to sew to perfection and enjoy the results.

Tammy's mother, Jean Young, encouraged her to sew at an early age and taught her about patterns, fabric, and combining all the elements for a fashionable wardrobe. Tammy's late grandmother, Maud MacKay, was also a positive influence, keeping continually busy with her handicrafts, including hooked and braided rugs, quilting, and sewing.

Special thanks to our friend and fellow author, sewing expert Gail Brown, who has inspired us to expand our serging horizons.

Thanks also to our incomparable illustrator, Chris Hansen, for his talent, hard work, and friendship. Finally, many thanks go to our series editor, Robbie Fanning, and to the entire Chilton team for their support, encouragement, and professionalism.

The following are registered trademark names used in this book: *Decor 6, Designer 6, Lycra, Scotch, Ultrasuede,* and *Velcro.*

# Preface

Have you ever gone shopping and come across a great item—a nightshirt, hair ornament, or unusual pillow, for example—and "just knew" you could make it for much less money? Sometimes for so much less, it's mind boggling.

You knew your serger could quickly duplicate many of the commercial construction techniques used, if only you had specific instructions. Most commercial patterns, even those with serger directions included, don't always tell you the fastest, easiest, and best ways to proceed.

Now you can make 48 easy projects, with clear step-by-step instructions, even if you're just a beginner or are apprehensive about using your serger. The projects are great time-savers for more experienced serging enthusiasts, too.

We're often asked the same questions over and over. One is, "How do you decide what to write about in each of your books?" This book was only a matter of responding to numerous requests for more simple serger projects. Because *ABCs of Serging* and *Serged Garments in Minutes* (see Other Books by the Authors in the back of this book) don't include projects, we felt that a project book reinforcing the information in those two books would be helpful. We begin with a review of serging basics, then feature one skill group in each chapter, from basic seams and edges through simple decorative serging.

"Which of your serging books should I buy first (or next)?" is another recurrent question. We suggest that any beginning serger user start with the basic *ABCs of Serging* book. *Simply Serge Any Project* is a companion to *ABCs* and includes projects to help you reinforce and practice those basic skills. If you want to learn more about constructing garments on your serger, *Serged Garments in Minutes* takes you through all of the basics and beyond. *Simply Serge Any Fabric* is a handy reference focusing on the special techniques necessary to serge all fabric types from batiste, silk, and knits to velvet, denim, and fake fur. *Distinctive Serger Gifts & Crafts* is a project book with totally different items, many more challenging than those in this book. The *Know Your Serger* series for specific brands concentrates on decorative serging from basic to advanced, and for these books you will need a prior knowledge of basic serging skills.

In talking to people around the country, we're frequently asked how we can work so closely together when Naomi lives in Springfield, Oregon, and Tammy lives in San Francisco. We take advantage of all the modern conveniences—phone, FAX, modem, and overnight shipping. In general, Tammy comes up with the ideas and outline, Naomi does most of the testing and instructions, and Tammy writes the final manuscript. But we're flexible: Naomi contributes some great ideas and Tammy does some testing, too.

Another common question is, "How do you select the projects?" We keep files of unusual items we see in magazines, catalogs, and other literature. Once in awhile, we dream something up that we think would be useful or interesting. In this book, Chapters 2 through 8 begin with at least two basic garments. The garments are followed by accessories, home decoration projects, and other useful items. The nongarment projects in each chapter are placed in order from the easiest and fastest to a little more challenging or time-consuming—none of the projects is hard. Some can be finished in a few minutes, while others many take an evening to complete.

We're frequently asked, "Why don't you give specific pattern numbers in your books?" The reason is that most pattern companies discard patterns on a regular basis and reissue similar styles under different numbers, so our books would have to be continually revised. The basic styles we have selected are always available and can be found from nearly all the pattern companies.

We hope you'll enjoy making the quick and easy items in *Serge a Simple Project*. They truly are fast, fun, and foolproof.

Tammy Young & Naomi Baker

# 1 Serging Simplified

Whether you're a novice serger user or simply haven't used yours to its fullest potential, a basic serging review can help you get better results and more enjoyment from this special machine.

Your serger will work side by side with your conventional sewing machine to give the most possible options. Use the sewing machine when top-stitching, edge-stitching, or straight-stitching is necessary on a project or garment. Use your serger to duplicate many factory techniques that the sewing machine cannot accomplish or cannot accomplish as easily, such as ravel-free finishing, speedy production methods, even pucker-free feeding, stretch seaming, and a wide range of decorative accents.

## SERGED STITCH TYPES

Most serger models have more than one stitch type. The most common stitch, available on practically every serger model, is the **3-thread overlock**, and it is the only one many people use for serging. You can use it for seaming, edge-finishing, flatlocking, and rolled edges. In a perfectly adjusted balanced 3-thread stitch, the needle thread forms a straight line and the looper threads lie flat on the top and underside, interlocking at the fabric edge. (Fig. 1–1)

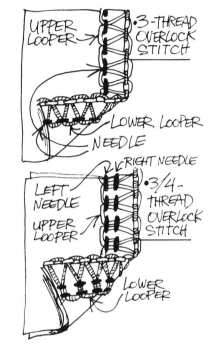

**Fig. 1-1** *Your serger will feature a combination of stitch types.*

Another popular stitch is the 3/4-thread overlock, which uses a second needle to add an extra row of stitching, making it a little more durable but less stretchy than the 3-thread stitch. This stitch is most commonly used for seaming, but you can also use it for novelty types of edge-finishing or flatlocking. By taking out either needle, you can convert the 3/4-thread stitch to a 3-thread, wider using the left needle and narrower using the right needle.

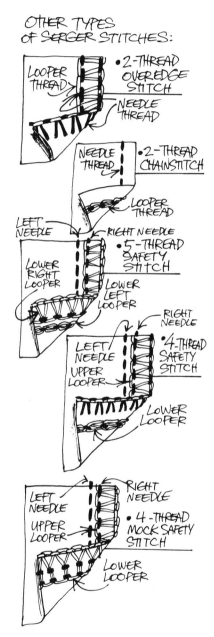

**Fig. 1-1 (cont.)**

Other types of serged stitches are also available, although no serger model will have all of them. These include:

## 2-THREAD OVEREDGE—

Using a needle thread and one looper thread, this stitch does not lock on the needleline, so it is not recommended for seaming. It is, however, an excellent option for lighter-weight edge-finishing, flatlocking, and rolled edges.

## 2-THREAD CHAINSTITCH—

A needle thread and a looper thread are also used for this stitch, but the looper thread stays on the underside and does not go over the edge. The stitch looks like a sewing machine straight-stitch on the right side of the fabric and has very little stretch.

## 5-THREAD SAFETY—

This is an extra-wide stitch created with two needles and three loopers, forming a combined 3-thread overlock and 2-thread chainstitch. It is used to serge very stable seams and edges, especially on loosely woven fabrics and on stress-prone areas. The stitch has little stretch and is used most often on draperies, other home decoration items, woven children's clothing, or sturdy work clothes.

## 4-THREAD SAFETY—

Combining the 2-thread overedge and the 2-thread chainstitch, this stitch uses two needles and two loopers, and serves the same functions as the 5-thread safety stitch but is just a little less sturdy.

## 4-THREAD MOCK SAFETY—

Available on only a few serger models, this stitch is similar to the 3/4-thread stitch, but the upper looper thread does not interlock with the left needle; therefore it can be converted to only a narrow 3-thread stitch, using the right needle and removing the left. The stitch does have moderate stretch and is used similarly to the 3/4-thread stitch.

## Special Serging Supplies

In addition to conventional sewing supplies, these serger-specific items will help you complete projects more quickly and easily:

- The accessories, attachments, owner's manual, and other information included with your machine.

- Chilton's *ABCs of Serging* and *Serged Garments in Minutes* books for more detailed explanations and additional information.

- Serger or all-purpose thread—one spool or cone for each needle and looper you will be using.

- Spare serger needles. Always use the ones recommended by your dealer. On many models, you will use a size 11/75 for lightweight and all-purpose serging and a size 14/90 for heavier fabric or when using heavier thread in the needle. If your machine uses a standard household needle, you can use a size 12/80 for all-purpose serging.

IF YOUR SERGER NEEDLE HAS ONE FLAT SIDE ON THE TOP OF THE SHANK, INSERT IT WITH THE FLAT SIDE TOWARD THE BACK OF THE MACHINE. IF THE NEEDLE HAS A ROUND SHANK, INSERT IT SO THE GROOVE AND EYE FACE DIRECTLY TO THE FRONT AND THE NEEDLE SCARF IS TOWARD THE BACK. ALWAYS BE SURE TO PUSH THE NEW NEEDLE COMPLETELY UP INTO THE NEEDLE BAR AND SCREW IT IN SECURELY OR YOUR STITCHES WON'T FORM PROPERLY. (FIG. 1-2)

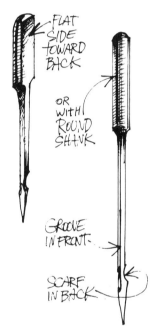

*Fig. 1-2 Always use a sharp new needle and insert it correctly, pushing it completely into the needle bar.*

- Needle-nose pliers or a needle inserter.

- Spare machine knife (if one isn't included with your machine accessories).

- Serger tweezers.

- Seam sealant.

- Transparent tape, such as *Scotch* brand.

- Loop turner or tapestry needle.

- Disappearing markers, both water-soluble and air-erasable.

For certain serger projects or for decorative serging, you will also find these notions helpful to keep on hand:

- Specialty thread, including woolly nylon, lightweight monofilament nylon, buttonhole twist, fusible thread, pearl rayon and cotton, and other decorative threads.

- Clear elastic—most helpful in 3/8″ (1cm) and 1/2″ (1.3cm) widths.

- Other elastic, from cording to wide sew-through waistband varieties.

- A supply of fusible interfacings in various weights.

- Velcro—3/4″ (2cm) and 1 1/2″ (4cm) widths are very handy.

- Glue stick.

- Craft glue or a hot glue gun.

- Polyester fiberfill.

# GETTING STARTED

Before you begin using your serger, take time to become familiar with it. Set it up, following your owner's manual, and read through the manual while sitting in front of the machine so the instructions will make more sense. Each serger model is a little different, so locate every feature on the machine and determine how it works.

## Threading Your Machine

Always use smooth, good-quality thread so it will stand up to the stress of high-speed serging. Before threading the machine, be sure the thread-guide pole is fully extended or the stitches will not form correctly.

Serger thread often comes on cones and the machine's cone holders will keep them stable on the spool pins. When using all-purpose thread, always put it on the spool pins with the notch down and use spool caps to help it feed evenly into the machine. (Fig. 1-3)

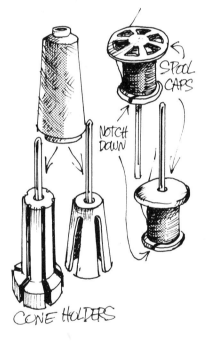

Fig. 1-3 Keep thread feeding evenly and smoothly by using your machine's special accessories.

To thread the serger, follow the instructions in your owner's manual (they may be printed on the machine as well). To help thread the looper eyes more easily, especially when using a specialty thread, use a needle threader, a drugstore-purchased dental-floss threader, or make a thread cradle using all-purpose thread. (Fig. 1-4)

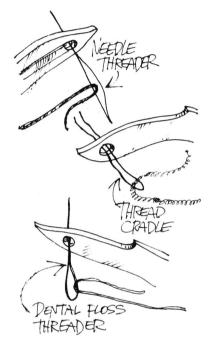

Fig. 1-4 Thread the looper eyes using one of these easy methods.

Changing to a different thread type or color need not be a lengthy, time-consuming process. Use this quick-change method for the best results:

1 Cut the needle thread(s) directly above the needle eye(s).

2 Hold the end of the thread chain and run out about 4″ (10cm) of unchained thread from the loopers. (Fig. 1-5)

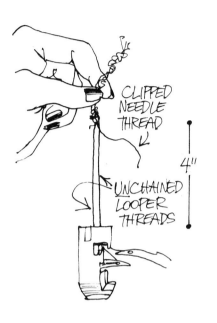

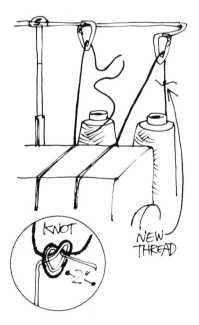

*Fig. 1-5 Quickly change thread by clipping the needle thread, running the other thread out a few inches, tying on the new thread, and pulling it through.*

3 Clip the thread or threads you want to change right above the spool or cone and replace with the new thread, securely tying the ends together in a simple overhand knot.

4 Adjust the tension to its lowest setting for the thread(s) you are changing, so the knot won't hang up or untie as you pull it through. Lift the presser foot and gently pull each thread you are replacing until the end is several inches past the foot.

**IF YOU ARE CHANGING TO A HEAVY THREAD, YOU MAY NEED TO TAKE IT COMPLETELY OUT OF THE TENSION MECHANISM IN ORDER TO PULL IT THROUGH. IF THE KNOT IS TOO LARGE TO FIT THROUGH THE LOOPER EYE, CUT IT OFF AND THREAD THE EYE MANUALLY.**

5 Rethread the needle(s), replace the thread complete-ly in the tension mecha-nism(s) if you removed it, return to the previous tension setting(s), and slowly begin serging to form a thread chain.

When a thread breaks or the machine is unthreaded, you must know how to thread the serger from scratch. The more you practice threading your machine, the easier it becomes, until you wonder why it seemed so intimidating. Follow these guidelines:

1 Consult your owner's manual to see which looper to thread first. Follow the thread path indicated, being sure to feed the thread through each guide and engaging it completely in the tension mechanism.

2 Next thread the other looper, following the same procedure. Before you thread the eye of the second looper, make sure the loopers are not crossed. (Fig. 1-6)

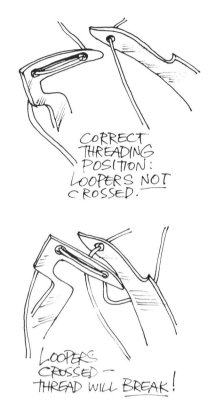

*Fig. 1-6 Be sure the loopers are not crossed before threading the second one.*

3 Turn the handwheel (in the direction indicated on your machine or in your manual) to be sure the two looper threads are not tangling. Then thread the needle(s) last, following the indicated thread path(s) and being sure the thread is completely in the tension mechanism.

4 Position all of the thread ends under the back of the presser foot before begin-ning to serge. They should run directly from the needle and looper eyes without crossing. (Fig. 1-7)

Fig. 1-7 *Before serging, draw the threads directly from the needle and looper eyes out and under the back of the presser foot.*

5 Lower the presser foot and begin serging slowly, checking to see if the stitches are forming over the stitch finger. Serge several inches of thread chain before beginning to serge on fabric.

IF THE STITCHES ARE NOT FORM-ING, THE SERGER IS PROBABLY NOT THREADED CORRECTLY. CAREFULLY TRACE EACH THREAD TO SEE THAT IT HAS BEEN FED CORRECTLY THROUGH EVERY GUIDE AND THROUGH THE EYE OF THE LOOPER AND NEEDLE WITHOUT CROSSING ANOTHER THREAD. CHECK TO SEE THAT THE THREAD UNWINDS SMOOTHLY FROM THE SPOOL OR CONE AND IS NOT WRAPPED AROUND THE SPOOL PIN, A THREAD GUIDE, OR THE NEEDLE. IF THERE IS STILL A PROBLEM, CLIP THE NEEDLE THREAD(S) JUST ABOVE THE EYE(S) AND TURN THE HAND-WHEEL UNTIL THE LOOPERS ARE NOT CROSSING. (SEE FIG. 1-6) HOLD THE LOOPER THREADS BEHIND THE PRESSER FOOT AND TURN THE HAND-WHEEL A FEW TIMES TO BE SURE THEY ARE NOT TANGLING. THEN RETHREAD THE NEEDLE(S).

## Stitching Accurately

When you begin serging on fabric, you need to know where to position the fabric edge. A wide 3-thread stitch is usually about $\frac{1}{4}$" (6mm) wide. If the seam allowance is $\frac{5}{8}$" (1.5cm), you will guide the fabric so the needle is on the seamline and the knives will trim off about $\frac{3}{8}$" (1cm). When you serge along the edge of the fabric, or when your pattern's seam allowances are $\frac{1}{4}$" (6mm), you won't want to trim any of the fabric with the knives, so hold the edge even with the right edge of the throat plate. (Fig. 1-8)

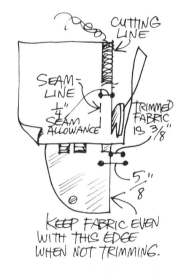

Fig. 1-8 *Guide the fabric so that any excess seam allowance will be trimmed off by the knives.*

Some models have markings on the front of the machine to help you guide the fabric edge accurately when you serge with a seam allowance of $\frac{1}{2}$" (1.3cm), $\frac{5}{8}$" (1.5cm), $\frac{3}{4}$" (2cm), or 1" (2.5cm). If not, put a piece of masking tape on your machine and mark the positions on it, measuring from the needle to the right. It is also helpful to mark the needle-line(s) on the top of the presser foot (if they are not there already) so you can guide the needle exactly where you want it. (Fig. 1-9)

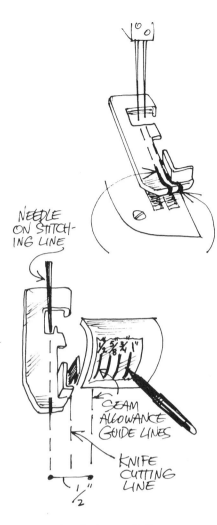

Fig. 1-9 *Mark the needleline position(s) on the foot and mark the fabric-edge guidelines on the machine front.*

When you begin to serge, always test your stitching on scraps of your project fabric to adjust and perfect the stitch you will be using. For practice as a beginner, use strips of medium-weight woven fabric. After you have serged a thread chain, feed the fabric under the presser foot. You'll find it is easiest to guide the fabric when you're trimming between $\frac{1}{8}$" (3mm) and $\frac{3}{8}$" (1cm) off the fabric edge, but you can trim more or less when necessary.

WHEN YOU ARE SERGING DIFFI-
CULT FABRIC THAT IS THICK, SLIP-
PERY, OR STRETCHY, OR WHEN
YOU ARE MATCHING A PATTERN,
BE SURE TO LIFT THE PRESSER
FOOT FIRST, POSITION THE
FABRIC JUST IN FRONT OF THE
KNIVES, AND LOWER THE FOOT
AGAIN BEFORE SERGING. THE
FOOT WILL ANCHOR THE FABRIC
IN POSITION.

To guide the fabric, place
your left hand to the left and
behind the presser foot. Place
your right hand in front of the
foot. The feed dogs will draw
the fabric through, so don't pull
it. (Fig. 1-10)

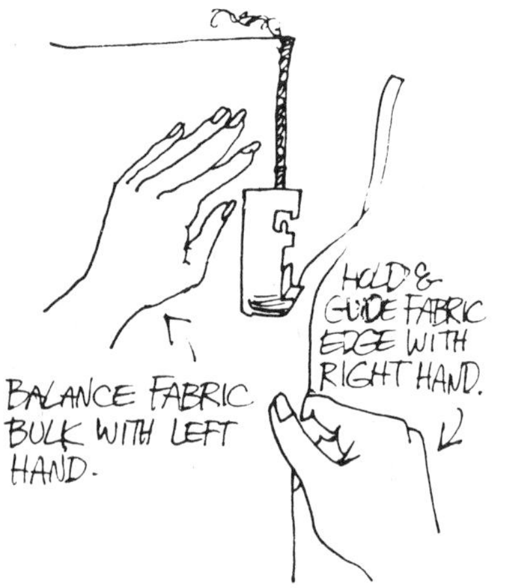

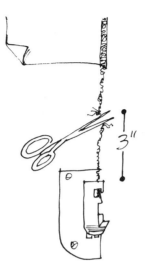

Fig. 1-10 *Hold the fabric with both
hands, but don't pull it through
under the foot.*

IN SOME CASES, ESPECIALLY
ON LIGHTWEIGHT OR STRETCHY
FABRIC, YOU WILL NEED TO
ANCHOR SEVERAL STITCHES IN
THE FABRIC, THEN HOLD THE
THREAD CHAIN TAUT BEHIND
THE PRESSER FOOT TO BEGIN
SMOOTHLY. THIS IS ANOTHER
REASON IT IS ALWAYS IMPORTANT
TO TEST ON SCRAPS OF YOUR
PROJECT FABRIC BEFORE BEGIN-
NING THE ACTUAL PROJECT.

When you reach the end of
the fabric, continue to serge for
several inches, leaving a thread
chain on the end to keep the
stitching from unraveling. This
is called "chaining off." Then
cut the threads by hand, leaving
at least 3″ (7.5cm) connected to
the machine. (Fig. 1-11)

Fig. 1-11 *Chain off at the fabric
edge and clip the middle of the
thread chain.*

## Making Tension Adjustments

One of the most confusing
and intimidating techniques in
using the serger is properly
adjusting the tensions. Once
you understand how to do this,
though, it's very logical and you
shouldn't have further problems. In fact, you will need to
understand tension adjustments
to convert to a rolled-edge or
flatlock stitch.

Follow these basic guidelines:

■ Turn a tension dial to the
right or a higher (plus)
setting to tighten the thread.
Turn it to the left or a lower
(minus) setting to loosen it.

IF YOUR MODEL HAS TENSION
KNOBS, USE THE JINGLE "RIGHTY
TIGHTY, LEFTY LOOSEY" TO
REMEMBER WHICH DIRECTION TO
TURN A KNOB. IF YOU CAN'T
REMEMBER THIS OR HAVE INSET
DIALS, PUT A PIECE OF MASKING
TAPE ON THE FRONT OF YOUR
MACHINE WITH A NOTE TO
REMIND YOURSELF: "HIGH =
TIGHTER, LOW = LOOSER."

■ On any balanced stitch, you
want the looper threads to
interlock right at the edge. If
one looper-thread tension is
too tight, it will pull the other
looper thread around the
edge of the fabric. (Fig. 1-12)

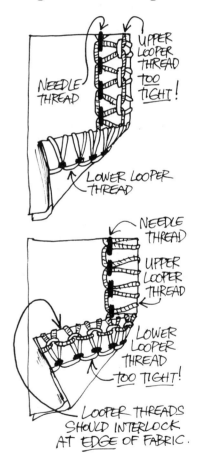

Fig. 1-12 *When the upper looper
thread is too tight, the lower looper
thread is pulled to the top side. When
the lower looper thread is too tight,
the upper looper thread is pulled to
the underside.*

- Always loosen the tension that is too tight first, to bring that thread to the exact edge of the fabric. If the stitches interlock off the fabric edge, both looper threads may be too loose and you will need to tighten them.

- Next, adjust the needle-thread tension—it should run in a straight line along the left side of the stitch. If the tension is too tight, the fabric will pucker at the seamline. If it is too loose, the stitches will spread open when the seamline is pressed open. (Fig. 1-13)

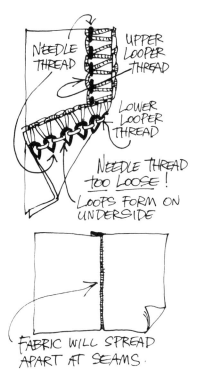

*Fig. 1-13 Adjust the needle-thread tension so the thread forms a straight line on both sides of the fabric.*

- Make only one adjustment at a time so you can see the results. Also make small adjustments, because only a fractional change can make a difference.

- Whenever you change the stitch length or width, the thread, or the fabric, you will likely need to change the tension. There are so many variables that simply keeping track of the numbers on the dial for a particular stitch doesn't always work. You'll often need looser tension for wider stitches, longer stitches, heavier thread, and thicker fabric. Conversely, you'll need tighter tension for narrower and shorter stitches, lightweight, slippery, or stretchy thread, and lighter-weight fabric.

YOU DON'T NEED TO REMEMBER ALL OF THESE GUIDELINES. SIMPLY TEST THE STITCH, SEE WHAT IT LOOKS LIKE, AND ADJUST ACCORDINGLY. REMEMBER TO FIRST LOOSEN ANY THREAD THAT IS TOO TIGHT. THEN IF A THREAD HANGS OFF THE EDGE OR THE NEEDLE THREAD ISN'T IN A STRAIGHT LINE, TIGHTEN IT.

## Changing the Stitch Size

All sergers can be adjusted in some way to change the stitch length and width—check your owner's manual for the correct adjustment procedures. (Fig. 1-14)

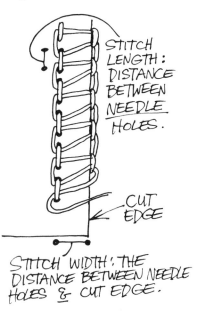

*Fig. 1-14 Learn how to change your serger's stitch width and length.*

Although the stitch-length capabilities can vary from one model to another, the maximum range is from less than 1mm to 4mm or 5mm. A normal serged stitch is about 3mm long. In general, you will need a longer stitch for heaver fabric and a shorter stitch for lighter fabric. Long stitches can cause lightweight fabric to pucker, but that can be an advantage when you are gathering. Short stitches can stretch or ruffle the edge on knits or bias fabric, but that can be useful when you want to lettuce the edge. Too short a stitch on delicate fabric can also weaken the seamline, so then, for durability, you will want to use a slightly longer stitch.

Depending on your serger model, you may have a full range of stitch-width options or only a few. In general, use a narrower stitch for lightweight fabric so it won't bunch under the stitching. Use a wider stitch for heavy or ravelly fabric for more durability.

*REMEMBER TO CHECK THE TENSION WHENEVER YOU CHANGE THE STITCH LENGTH OR WIDTH, AND ADJUST IT IF NECESSARY. A NARROWER OR SHORTER STITCH NEEDS LESS THREAD, SO IT REQUIRES TIGHTER LOOPER-THREAD TENSIONS. A WIDER OR LONGER STITCH NEEDS MORE THREAD AND REQUIRES LOOSER TENSIONS. (FIG. 1-15)*

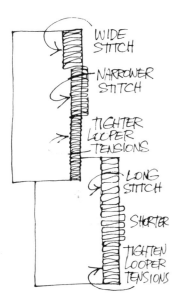

Fig. 1-15 *Adjust the looper-thread tension when you change the stitch size.*

## Using Differential Feed

One of the handiest serger features that has been developed in recent years is the differential feed. It is available on many serger models and regulates the amount of tension placed on the fabric as it is serged over.

Machines with differential feed have one set of feed dogs under the front of the presser foot and one under the back. They can be adjusted, by setting the differential feed, to take longer or shorter strokes either to ease or stretch the fabric as it feeds under the foot. (Fig. 1-16)

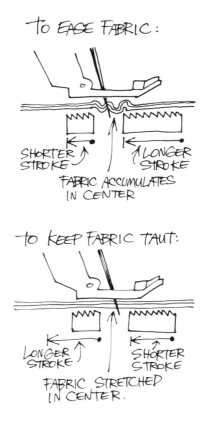

Fig. 1-16 *Use a higher differential-feed setting to ease fabric and a lower setting to hold it taut.*

With a 1.0 or N (normal) setting, the feed dogs move the same amount and no pressure is put on the fabric. To ease or gather the fabric and prevent stretching it, use a setting higher than normal. To hold the fabric taut and prevent puckering on silky or lightweight fabrics or to help stretch the fabric for lettucing, use a setting lower than normal.

*IF YOU HAVE TROUBLE REMEMBERING WHICH DIRECTION TO SET THE DIFFERENTIAL FEED LEVER OR DIAL, PUT A NOTE ON MASKING TAPE NEXT TO IT: "HIGH = EASING, LOW = TAUT."*

If your machine does not have differential feed, you can duplicate the results manually. To ease the fabric and eliminate stretching, ease-plus. Gently push the fabric under the front of the presser foot with your right hand and use your left index finger to slow down the exit from under the back of the foot. It's also helpful to lengthen the stitch. (Fig. 1-17)

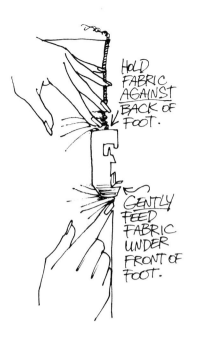

Fig. 1-17 *Ease-plus to replicate a higher differential feed setting.*

Use taut serging to prevent puckering and help fabric layers feed evenly. Apply an equal amount of pressure to the fabric as it feeds under the foot, but do not pull the fabric through the machine. (Fig. 1-18)

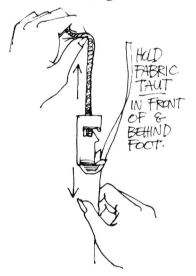

Fig. 1-18 *Prevent puckering by holding the fabric taut manually.*

# HANDY SERGING TECHNIQUES

Serging has several unique characteristics that differ from conventional sewing. The presser foot is larger and holds the fabric more firmly, but it reduces visibility as the stitch is being made. Most serging must be done on a fold or edge and the serged stitch itself is considerably different than a conventional straight-stitch.

## Preparing a Seam

It isn't always necessary to pin layers of fabric together before seaming, because the larger presser foot will help hold them in place. However, when the fabric is slippery or the seam is more complicated, you can use pins.

Be sure to keep pins away from the serger knives as well as the needle—they can cause major damage. In most cases, position them parallel to the stitching line and about ½″ (1.3cm) to the left. (Fig. 1-19)

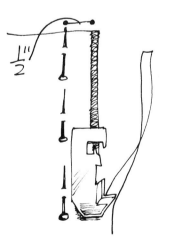

Fig. 1-19 *Position pins so the serger knives won't hit them.*

On a tricky area, such as a pleat or a tuck, you might need to pin across the stitching line to hold the fabric in place. In this case, use pins with large heads and **concentrate**, removing each pin before it reaches the presser foot.

On a straight seam, even a long one, you usually will not need to pin. Simply anchor a couple of stitches in the fabric, then "finger-pin" by holding the remainder of the edge together with your fingers as you complete the seam.

We seldom baste a seam before serging, but will pin-fit instead. The one exception is when matching a tricky stripe. Then we sometimes use a glue stick to align the layers perfectly before serging them together.

## Serging Curves and Corners

In most cases, you will serge an outside corner by chaining off the edge, pivoting the fabric, and serging back on the adjoining edge. You can trim the fabric while serging or just skim the edge with the knives (Fig. 1-20)

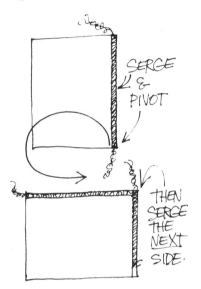

*Fig. 1-20 Serge neat outside corners by chaining off the edge and serging back on the adjoining one.*

Inside corners must be handled differently. It is easier to pretrim any extra seam allowance so you'll be just skimming the fabric edge with the knives. Serge along one edge, stopping when the knives are about ½″ (1.3cm) from the corner, with the needle down. Raise the presser foot, pull the fabric edge into a straight line in front of the foot, lower the foot, and continue serging. As you serge across the corner point, push the fabric to the right with your index finger, making sure the stitching catches the fabric. (Fig. 1-21)

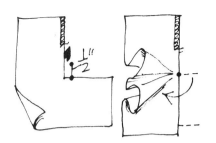

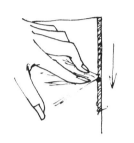

*Fig. 1-21 Stop serging before the knives reach an inside corner and pull the fabric in a straight line in front of the foot before continuing to serge the edge.*

**USE THIS SAME TECHNIQUE FOR SERGING A SLIT. YOU WON'T NEED TO PRETRIM THE EDGES, JUST PULL THEM INTO A STRAIGHT LINE IN FRONT OF THE PRESSER FOOT BEFORE YOU SERGE OVER THE CORNER POINT.**

When you serge a curved edge, use a similar technique, pulling the fabric in a straight line in front of the presser foot to keep the stitching uniform on the edge of the fabric. For an outside curve, you'll be pulling the fabric to the right in front of the foot to keep it in a straight line. On an inside curve, you'll be pulling the fabric to the left. **Serge slowly.** (Fig. 1-22)

*Fig. 1-22 Guide a curved edge by pulling it straight in front of the foot before feeding it underneath.*

## Beginning and Ending in the Middle of an Edge

When serging a rounded edge, or when you want to leave an opening along one edge to turn and/or stuff a project, you will need to begin serging in the middle of an edge. Although you can simply angle on and off the fabric, the results are not as neat.

To begin serging directly on the seamline, you must first trim away any excess seam allowance. Then clear the stitch finger by raising the presser foot and the needle, pulling a slight amount of slack in the needle thread, and gently pulling the thread chain toward the back until the stitches slip off the stitch finger. (Fig. 1-23)

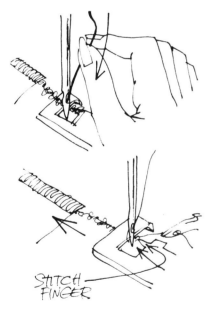

STITCH FINGER

**Fig. 1-23** *Clear the stitch finger by pulling slack in the needle thread, then slip the stitches off toward the back.*

*IF YOUR MODEL HAS A TENSION RELEASE FEATURE, SIMPLY USE IT INSTEAD OF PULLING SLACK IN THE NEEDLE THREAD.*

To neatly complete a rounded edge, simply lap the ending stitches at least ½" (1.3cm) over the beginning stitches, being careful not to cut them with the knives. Again remove the stitches from the stitch finger and pull the fabric away from the machine.

*A QUICK WAY TO CHAIN OFF NEATLY WITHOUT PUTTING ANOTHER STITCH IN THE FABRIC IS TO RAISE THE NEEDLE AND PRESSER FOOT, PULL THE FABRIC BEHIND THE NEEDLE, AND THEN CONTINUE TO SERGE. (FIG. 1-24)*

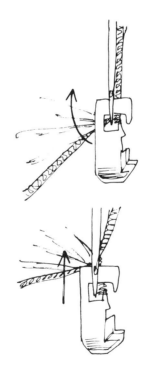

**Fig. 1-24** *Chain off neatly by lifting the needle and presser foot, pulling the fabric behind the needle, then continue to serge.*

Sometimes you will want to correct a section of uneven stitching or close an opening where the stitching will be visible. Use the same techniques for beginning and ending as you do for the rounded edge:

1. Pretrim any excess seam allowance. If you are correcting uneven serged stitching, trim away the thread in the imperfect section. If you are leaving an opening, begin and end as you would for a rounded edge, above, but leave an opening instead of lapping.

2. Clear the stitch finger and lower the needle into the seamline about ½" (1.3cm) before the end of the previous serging.

3. Serge the unstitched area, ending about ½" (1.3cm) past the beginning of the previous serging. Guide the fabric so the needlelines match on both layers of stitching, but be careful not to cut the threads on the first layer.

4. Raise the presser foot and the needle, pull the fabric behind the needle, and chain off. (See Fig. 1-24)

5. Use one of the following methods to secure the loose thread chains.

## Securing Stitches

With some thread, such as woolly nylon, and a short stitch length, you won't need to secure the thread chain ends after lapping the serging. And often the end of a seam will be crossed by other stitching and won't have to be secured. However, in many cases, you will need to secure the end of serged stitching to ensure that it won't unravel.

The easiest method is to dab a small drop of seam sealant on the end of the stitching and clip the excess thread chain when it dries. Another quick method is to knot the end of the thread chain before clipping the excess, or use both methods together. (Fig. 1-25)

WHEN YOU ARE SERGING A GARMENT IN WHICH THE SECURED THREAD-CHAIN END WILL BE WORN NEXT TO THE SKIN, DO NOT USE SEAM SEALANT. IT HARDENS WHEN DRY AND CAN CAUSE IRRITATION.

Another common method of securing thread-chain ends is to use a loop turner or tapestry needle, threading the loose end back through the stitching on the underside of the fabric. (Fig. 1-26)

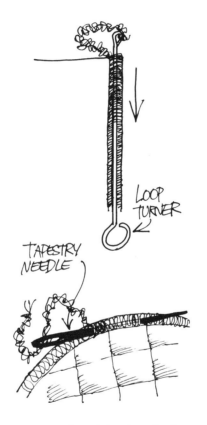

LOOP TURNER

TAPESTRY NEEDLE

**Fig. 1-26** *Thread the chain back under the stitches and clip away the excess.*

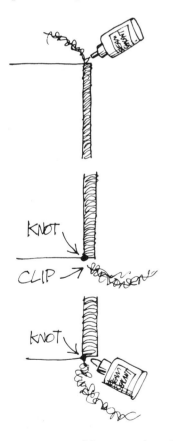

KNOT

CLIP →

KNOT

**Fig. 1-25** *Quickly secure thread-chain ends by using seam sealant, knotting, or both, then clip away the excess.*

## Removing Serged Stitches

When you need to remove serged stitching, you can quickly serge again, trimming off the original stitching with the knives, but that will make your project or garment a little smaller. You can also use a seam ripper, cutting through the looper thread on one side of the fabric and pulling out all of the cut thread pieces.

The easiest way to remove balanced serged stitching, though, is to pull the needle thread (or both threads if you used two needles):

1 Clip off the thread chain at one end of the stitching. Smooth out the thread chain at the opposite end and find the shortest thread (which is the needle thread).

2 Gently pull the thread, gathering the fabric and sliding the thread along through the stitches. (Fig. 1-27)

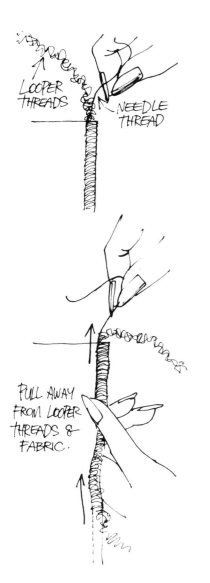

**Fig. 1-27** *Find the shortest thread, the needle thread, and pull it to remove the serged stitching.*

3 The looper threads will pull away easily after the needle thread is completely removed and no longer holding them in place.

### Pressing Serged Seams

After you have serged a seam, press the stitching flat. Then press the seam flat with the allowance to one side so it will be in position when crossed by another seam or row of edge-finishing. (Fig. 1-28)

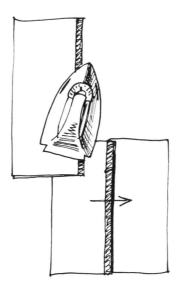

**Fig. 1-28** *Press the stitching flat before pressing the seam flat with the allowance to one side.*

# SERGING ROLLED EDGES

The rolled edge is a simple and popular stitch on the serger. It is used as a narrow, corded-like finish on everything from napkins and craft projects to everyday clothing and formal wear.

Any 3-thread stitch can be adjusted to a rolled edge by using a short to medium-length, narrow stitch and tightening the lower looper-thread tension. The tightened tension pulls the upper looper thread completely around the edge to the stitching line on the underside and the fabric edge rolls inside the stitch. (Fig. 1-29)

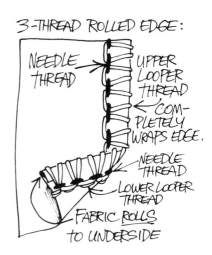

**Fig. 1-29** *Perfect a rolled-edge stitch for myriad uses.*

Consult your owner's manual on how to adjust your model for a rolled edge. On some you will need to change the presser foot and/or needle plate. You will also need to remove one needle if you are using two. Adjust to a short to medium-length, narrow stitch and tighten the lower looper-thread tension almost completely, then test the stitch.

- If the upper looper thread is not wrapping completely around the fabric edge, tighten the lower looper-thread tension even more.

- If it still isn't wrapping completely, slightly loosen the upper looper-thread tension.

- If the fabric is puckering along the needleline, loosen the needle-thread tension slightly.

- Continue testing and adjusting until the upper looper thread wraps the edge completely and the lower looper thread forms a straight line on the underside along the needleline.

IF YOUR SERGER MODEL HAS A 2-THREAD OVEREDGE STITCH, CHECK YOUR OWNER'S MANUAL FOR INSTRUCTIONS ON ADJUSTING IT TO A ROLLED EDGE.

# FLATLOCKING BASICS

Flatlocking is another handy serger stitch. It can be used for bulk-free seaming or for serging decoratively over folds. The stitch is also used for attaching trim or ribbon on top of fabric by seaming it over a folded edge.

Adjust for a 3-thread flatlock by starting with a wide, short- to medium-length balanced stitch. Then loosen the needle tension almost completely and tighten the lower looper-thread tension until the thread forms a straight line on the underside of the fabric. The upper looper-thread tension will usually not need to be adjusted. (Fig. 1-30)

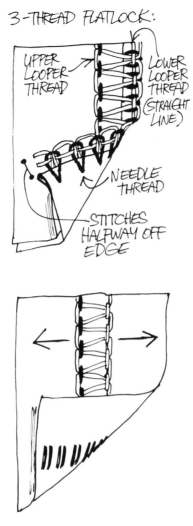

*Fig. 1-30 Pull the fabric in opposite directions to flatten the stitches after serging.*

To test the stitch, flatlock over a seam or edge with the stitches hanging halfway off the fabric. (Remember that because you will be guiding the fabric away from the knives to let the stitches hang off, you must pretrim any excess seam allowance.) Then gently pull the fabric and stitching flat. On a seam, the fabric edges should meet in the center under the stitches. On a fold, the fabric should flatten out completely under the flatlocking.

When you serge a flatlock stitch on the right side of the fabric with wrong sides together, the looped side of the stitch will show on the right side. When you flatlock from the wrong side with the fabric right sides together, the ladder side will show on the right side. Remember that the fabric side that is exposed when you flat-lock is the side where the loops (upper looper thread) will be.

IF YOUR SERGER MODEL HAS A 2-THREAD OVEREDGE STITCH, YOU CAN USE IT FOR FLATLOCKING WITHOUT MAKING ANY TENSION ADJUSTMENTS. SIMPLY SERGE A SEAM OR A FOLD WITH A WIDE, BALANCED STITCH AND PULL THE FABRIC FLAT.

## PURCHASING A SERGER

Since sergers were introduced to the consumer market, manufacturers have added numerous helpful features, so serging has become easier and easier. Before you purchase a serger, decide what you will be using it for—seam finishing, decorative techniques, dressmaking, home dec, draperies, or all-purpose serging? For the best value, purchase a serger not for what you may need someday but for what you will use now. In general, the more stitch types a machine offers, the more complicated it may be to use.

Begin looking for a serger by shopping the dealers in your area. The relationship you establish with your local dealer will be invaluable for regular serger maintenance and repair, education, techniques and ideas, and word on new accessories and notions. Many serger brands are comparable, but the dealer makes the difference. A knowledgeable, friendly, helpful, and inspiring dealer will be one of your greatest serging assets.

Try out the sergers you're most interested in. The dealer can help you select the models that will meet your specific needs—don't just look at the top-of-the-line machines. Take along swatches of the types of fabric you'll be using most and actually test each machine yourself. Also take along and test decorative thread if you'll be doing a lot of decorative serging. If you don't know how to serge, ask the dealer to help you. Then purchase the model you are most comfortable using that will accomplish the projects you intend to work on.

## IMPORTANT SERGER MAINTENANCE

Keep your serger in good working order to get maximum results and the longest life from it. Here's how:

- Make a habit of cleaning the lint and trimmings from your machine after every project.

- Change the needle(s) after every third project or when you begin to serge on delicate fabric—and be sure to insert them properly (see page 2).

- If your model requires oiling, oil the machine after every 12 to 15 hours of serging or when you haven't used it for some time.

- Check the knives and clean the machine thoroughly once a month.

- At least once a year, take your serger to the dealer for a timing and maintenance check—it's a finely tuned machine, much like an automobile, and needs the expert attention.

# 2 Basic Seams & Edges

Any 3- or 3/4-thread serger (or a serger that has these stitches as an option) is capable of neatly sewing basic seams and edges. Although other serger stitches can be used for seaming, these are the most versatile for everyday projects. The weight and weave of the fabric and the project itself will help determine which type of seam to use. You can simply serge a seam or you may choose to serge-finish the allowance of a conventional straight-stitched seam. Serge-finished edges can be turned and top-stitched to create a hem or they can be decoratively exposed on the right side. The projects in this chapter let you practice a variety of these basic techniques. (Fig. 2-1)

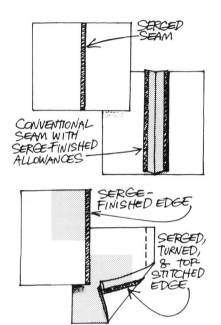

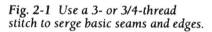

*Fig. 2-1 Use a 3- or 3/4-thread stitch to serge basic seams and edges.*

Before you begin, let's review the fundamentals that were discussed in detail in *ABCs of Serging:*

- Plan ahead. If you're making a garment, be sure the fit is correct before serge-seaming. Transfer any markings by using a disappearing marker on the wrong side of the fabric (because notches will be trimmed off by serge-finishing or serge-seaming). Decide how you will pin or baste the seams before sewing them (see page 9).

- Test first before serging on the project to be sure the machine is adjusted correctly.

- Line up the raw edge or edges with the seam allowance marking or line up the seamline with the left needleline mark on the presser foot (see page 5).

- Begin serging slowly and check the fabric every few inches to be sure both layers are flat.

- If the edge stretches out as you serge over it, use a higher differential feed setting or ease-plus. If the edge puckers, use a lower differential feed setting or taut serging (see pages 8 and 9).

- Leave several inches of thread chain at the beginning and end of the serged seams or edges to prevent the stitches from pulling apart before you serge over the ends or secure them by another method (see page 12).

- To save time, continuously serge as many seams and edges as you can without raising the presser foot. Leave at least 4″ of thread chain between each seam or edge and clip the middle of the loose thread chains to separate the sections.

- After serge-seaming, press the stitching flat, then press the seam flat with the allowance to one side.

NECKLINE LARGE ENOUGH TO PULL OVER HEAD

CAP OR CUT-ON SLEEVES

LOOSE FIT

## SUPER-SIMPLE PULLOVER TOP

Quickly make a simple shell using serge-seaming and serge-finishing. The shell is so easy to make that you can whip out several in one evening! (Fig. 2-2)

### SKILLS USED:

Serged seams; serge-finished edges; serged, turned, and top-stitched hems.

## Materials needed:

◆ Loose-fitting pullover top pattern with a faced neckline, cap or cut-on sleeves, and ⅝″ (1.5cm) seam allowances

◆ Light- to medium-weight knit or tightly woven fabric, following the pattern yardage requirements

*Fig. 2-2  Serge a basic pullover top in minutes.*

◆ Fusible interfacing for the neckline facing

◆ Matching serger or all-purpose thread for serging; matching all-purpose thread for the sewing machine

*IF YOU DON'T HAVE THREE OR FOUR SPOOLS OR CONES OF MATCHING THREAD, USE MATCHING THREAD IN THE NEEDLE (THE LEFT NEEDLE OF A 3/4-THREAD SERGER) AND A BLENDING COLOR IN THE LOOPERS. THE NEEDLE THREAD AT THE SEAMLINE WILL BE THE ONLY THREAD VISIBLE ON THE RIGHT SIDE OF THE GARMENT.*

## Cutting directions:

■ Make alterations if necessary. Because serge-seaming allows for minimum alteration, it is important to fit the pattern to your measurements before cutting the top. Compare your bust and hip measurements to those on the back of the pattern envelope and adjust the pattern accordingly. Many patterns include the actual bust and hip measurements on the pattern-front pieces themselves. If you are unsure of the fit after measuring, cut out the garment with wider 1″ seam allowances. Then pin-fit or machine-baste the garment together and check the fit before serge-seaming.

*USE A MULTISIZED PATTERN TO MAKE ALTERATIONS EASIER— TAPER GRADUALLY FROM ONE SIZE AT THE BUSTLINE, FOR EXAMPLE, TO ANOTHER SIZE AT THE WAISTLINE OR HIP.*

■ Cut the front, back, and facing pieces from the fabric.

■ Cut the facing pieces from the fusible interfacing.

■ Transfer the pattern markings to the wrong side of the fabric with a disappearing marker.

*BECAUSE YOUR PATTERN HAS 5/8″ (1.5CM) SEAM ALLOWANCES AND YOU WILL BE SERGE-SEAMING, YOU MAY CHOOSE TO MARK THE NOTCHES BY SNIPPING ABOUT 1/8″ (3MM) INTO THE SEAM ALLOWANCE AT THE POINT OF THE NOTCH. THIS TECHNIQUE CAN BE USED WHEN YOU NEED THE MARK ONLY TO LINE UP A SERGED SEAM AND WHEN THE ALLOWANCE IS WIDE ENOUGH THAT THE SNIP WILL BE TRIMMED OFF DURING SERGING.*

**SERGER SETTINGS:**

3- or 3/4-thread balanced stitch

**Stitch length:** Medium

**Stitch width:** Medium for lightweight fabrics; wide for loosely woven and knit fabrics

**Needle:** Size 11/75

*TO PREVENT HOLES OR SNAGS IN THE FABRIC, USE A NEW NEEDLE WHEN SERGING ON KNITS OR SILKIES.*

## How-tos:

1 Fuse the interfacing to the wrong side of the facing pieces, following the manufacturer's instructions.

2 Place the interfaced facing pieces right sides together and serge the shoulder seams. Begin by serging a few inches of thread chain, then place the two fabric layers under the presser foot. Serge-seam, trimming approximately ³/₈" (1cm) of the seam allowances, beginning at the outer facing edge of one shoulder and serging to the neckline. Without cutting, serge off the fabric for several inches and then serge back on at the seam on the opposite neckline edge and complete the second seam to the outer edge of the facing. Serge off, leaving a thread chain several inches long and press the seam allowance toward the front facing. (Fig. 2-3)

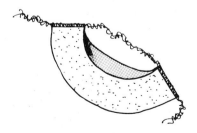

*Fig. 2-3 Continuously serge-seam the front and back neckline facings together.*

*FOR THE FLATTEST FINISH, STRAIGHT-STITCH THE FACING SHOULDER SEAMS AND PRESS THEM OPEN. IT IS NOT NECESSARY TO SERGE-FINISH THE EDGES OF THE SEAM ALLOWANCES.*

3 Raise the needle and the presser foot and pull the thread chain gently toward the back of the presser foot. Clear the stitch finger (see page 11 and Fig. 1-23) and separate the threads. With the facing right side up, place the outer edge of one shoulder seam under the presser foot, with the raw edge next to the knife. Serge-finish the outer edge, trimming only enough to neaten it. Lap the beginning stitches for about ¼" (6mm) before clearing the stitch finger again and gently pulling the fabric away from the presser foot.

*TO AVOID CUTTING THE BEGINNING STITCHES, MOVE THE FACING EDGE SLIGHTLY TO THE LEFT AS THE KNIVES REACH THE BEGINNING STITCHES. NEATLY OVERLAP THE STITCHING BY TURNING THE HANDWHEEL SLOWLY.*

4 Place the front and back sections right sides together at the shoulders and pin, positioning the pins parallel to and about ½" (1.3cm) inside the seamline at 1¹/₈" (2.8cm) to avoid the knives. (Fig. 2-4)

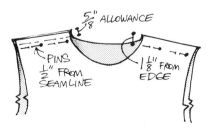

*Fig. 2-4 Pin the shoulder seams outside the stitching area before trying on the top and serge-seaming.*

*AT THIS POINT, MAKE SURE THE TOP WILL FIT OVER YOUR HEAD BY SLIPPING IT ON. KEEP IN MIND THAT APPROXIMATELY 3/8"(1CM) OF THE SEAM ALLOWANCE WILL BE TRIMMED AWAY, MAKING THE NECKLINE OPENING LARGER.*

5 Serge-seam the shoulders, beginning at one outer edge, serging continuously off the fabric at the neckline edge, back on at the opposite neckline edge, and off again at the outer sleeve edge. Press the seam flat and then press the seam allowances toward the garment back.

*WHEN USING LIGHTWEIGHT OR SILKY FABRIC, PREVENT PUCKERING WHILE SERGE-SEAMING BY ADJUSTING THE DIFFERENTIAL FEED TO ITS LOWEST SETTING. ALSO HOLD THE FABRIC TAUT IN FRONT OF AND BEHIND THE PRESSER FOOT.*

6 Pin the facing and the garment right sides together, matching the shoulder seams, and straight-stitch the neckline seam. Carefully trim the seam allowances to ¼" (6mm), clipping the curves. Press the allowances toward the facing. From the right side, under-stitch the facing just to the right of the seamline, catching the seam allowance on the underside.

7 Press the facing to the wrong side and pin it to the garment at the shoulder seams. From the right side, stitch-in-the-ditch of the shoulder seams, securing the facing underneath.

8 From the right side, serge-finish the sleeve hem edges, being careful not to stretch while serging. Press the sleeve hem allowances to the wrong side.

9 Pin the back to the front at one side/sleeve seam, opening out the hem allowance and positioning the pins about ¹/₂″ (1.3cm) inside the stitching line. Begin serge-seaming at the lower edge, keeping the edges in a straight line and stretching slightly as you seam the underarm. Press the seam allowance toward the back. (Fig. 2-5)

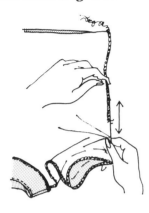

*Fig. 2-5 Hold the underarm curve straight and stretch slightly as you serge over it.*

**STRETCHING THE UNDERARM SEAM AS YOU SERGE ELIMINATES THE NEED TO REINFORCE THE CURVE.**

10 Serge-finish the lower hem edge from the right side of the fabric.

11 Beginning at the lower edge, serge-seam the other side/sleeve seam, following the instructions in step 9.

12 Finish the seam ends at the sleeve and lower edges by tying a knot in the thread chain close to the seam end. Clip the excess thread chain. (See Fig. 1-25)

13 Press the lower hem allowance to the wrong side. Hem the sleeves and lower edge by top-stitching from the right side.

*Fig. 2-6 Select a simple pull-on skirt pattern.*

# SPEEDY PULL-ON SKIRT

Serge this easy pull-on skirt in an hour to wear with the previous super-simple pullover top or other wardrobe favorites. The instructions feature pressed open, serge-finished seam allowances for a flatter finish. (Fig. 2-6)

### SKILLS USED:

Conventional seams with serge-finished allowances; serge-finished edges; serged, turned, and top-stitched hem.

## Materials needed:

- Loose-fitting pull-on straight skirt pattern with no pockets or with side-seam pockets that can be easily eliminated, inserted-elastic waistline, and ⁵/₈″ (1.5cm) seam allowances

- Medium-weight knit or tightly woven fabric, following the pattern yardage requirements

- Elastic equal to the length of your waist measurement and the width called for in the pattern. (See the "Elastic Selections Guidelines" chart on page 81 in *Serged Garments in Minutes* if you're unsure of which type to buy for any project.)

FOR EASE IN INSERTION, SUBSTI-TUTE A WIDER-WIDTH ELASTIC FOR MULTIPLE ROWS OF A NAR-ROWER WIDTH. FOR EXAMPLE, IF THE PATTERN REQUIRES TWO ROWS OF 1/2"-WIDE (1.3CM) ELASTIC, SUBSTITUTE ONE ROW OF 1 1/4"-WIDE (3CM) ELASTIC.

- Matching serger or all-purpose thread for serging; matching all-purpose thread for the sewing machine

IF YOU DON'T HAVE THREE OR FOUR CONES OR SPOOLS OF MATCHING THREAD, USE MATCHING THREAD IN THE SEAMLINE NEEDLE.

## Cutting directions:

- Make alterations if necessary. Before cutting out the skirt, it is important to fit the pattern to your hip measurement, allowing a minimum 3" (7.5cm) of ease. Compare your hip measurement and skirt length to the back of the pattern envelope and adjust the pattern accordingly. Many patterns include hip measurements on the pattern-front pieces themselves. If you are unsure of the fit after measuring, cut wider 1" (2.5cm) seam allowances. Then pin-fit or machine-baste the garment together and try it on before seaming.

- Cut the front and back skirt pieces from the fabric. If the pattern has pockets, eliminate them.

- Stretch the elastic comfortably around your waist, overlapping the ends 1/2" (1.3cm), and cut to that measurement (or mark the measurement and cut the excess after completing step 6).

SERGER SETTINGS:

3-thread balanced stitch

**Stitch length:** Medium

**Stitch width:** Medium

**Needle:** Size 11/75

TO AVOID MAKING HOLES IN THE FABRIC, USE A NEW NEEDLE WHEN SEWING KNITS.

## How-tos:

1 From the right side of the fabric, serge-finish the side-seam allowances of the front and back skirt pieces, leaving a thread chain on each end. When serging, just barely skim the edges to neaten them. If the fabric is trimmed, the skirt will be smaller than intended.

2 Place the front and back right sides together, matching the upper and lower edges and pinning one side into position. Straight-stitch using a 5/8" (1.5cm) seam allowance. Press the seam flat and then press it open. (Fig. 2-7)

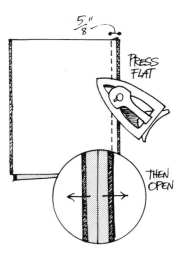

*Fig. 2-7 After seaming one side, press the serge-finished allowances.*

TO AVOID SHOW-THROUGH OF THE SEAM ALLOWANCES ON THE RIGHT SIDE OF THE FABRIC, PLACE PIECES OF WHITE OR BROWN PAPER UNDER THE ALLOWANCES AS YOU PRESS THE SEAM OPEN.

3 Serge-finish the skirt's upper and lower edges from the right side of the fabric, leaving a thread chain at each end.

4 Repeat step 2 for the opposite side of the skirt. Press the waistline casing and the hem allowance to the wrong side.

5 From the wrong side, beginning close to one side seam, top-stitch the waistline casing through the center of the serge-finished edge. Leave about 2″ (5cm) unstitched to insert the elastic.

6 Thread the elastic through the opening, pinning the final end to prevent it from being pulled into the casing. Make sure the elastic is not twisted in the casing, then lap the ends ¹/₂″ (1.3cm) and zigzag them together securely. (Fig. 2-8)

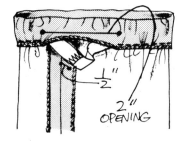

**Fig. 2-8** *Lap and zigzag the elastic ends.*

7 Top-stitch the opening closed. Stretch and release the elastic to distribute it evenly in the casing. From the right side, stitch-in-the-ditch of the side seams to keep the elastic from twisting.

8 Hand-stitch the hem in place.

# TWO-TONE THROW PILLOW

Serge-finished flanges accent this ultra-simple decorator pillow. (Fig. 2-9)

**SKILLS USED:**

Serge-finished edges.

## Materials needed:

◆ One square of medium- to heavy-weight woven cotton or cotton blend with no definite right or wrong side, 4″ (10cm) larger than the pillow form

◆ One square of the same fabric in a contrasting color

◆ One square pillow form

◆ An air-erasable marker

◆ Three cones or spools of all-purpose thread to match both square colors

**Fig. 2-9** *This pillow is so quick and easy that you can make a pile of them in one session.*

**SERGER SETTINGS:**

3-thread balanced stitch

**Stitch length:** Short (satin)

**Stitch width:** Narrow (use the right needle of a 3/4-thread machine)

**Needle:** Size 11/75

## How-tos:

1 From the right side, serge-finish the two lengthwise edges of one square with the thread color that matches the second square, leaving a thread chain on each end.

*WHEN YOU ADJUST FOR A SHORT NARROW STITCH, YOU MUST TIGHTEN THE UPPER AND LOWER LOOPER TENSIONS SO THAT THE THREADS OVERLOCK ON THE CUT EDGE. IF YOU CAN'T TIGHTEN THE TENSIONS ENOUGH, TRY WIDENING THE STITCH SLIGHTLY SO THE FABRIC WILL FILL THE SERGED STITCHES COMPLETELY.*

2 Serge-finish the opposite edges. Dab seam sealant on the corners and clip the thread chain when dry.

3 Repeat for the second square, using the contrasting thread color that matches the first square.

4 Pin the squares wrong sides together and, using the marker, lightly draw the pillow outline, centering it and leaving equal-size borders.

5 Straight-stitch three sides of the pillow on the marked lines and for 1″ (2.5cm) on both ends of the remaining side. Back-stitch. (Fig. 2-10)

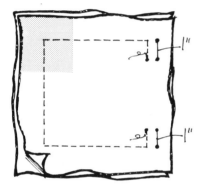

*Fig. 2-10 On the final side, leave a large opening to insert the pillow form.*

6 Insert the pillow form and carefully pin the opening closed on the marked line. Using a zipper foot, straight-stitch the opening closed, removing the pins before you reach them.

*YOU MAY USE POLYESTER FIBERFILL INSTEAD OF A PILLOW FORM. DETERMINE THE PILLOW SIZE AND CUT THE FABRIC TO THAT MEASUREMENT, ADDING 2″ (5CM) BORDERS ON ALL SIDES. COMPLETE THE PILLOW THROUGH STEP 5, LEAVING APPROXIMATELY 5″ (12.5CM) OPEN FOR STUFFING. STUFF EVENLY WITH THE FIBERFILL AND STRAIGHT-STITCH THE OPENING CLOSED.*

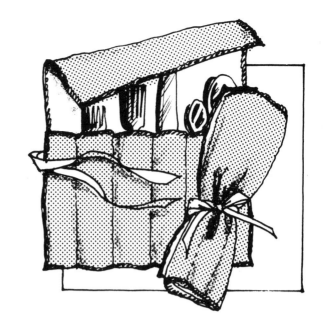

# SILVERWARE STORAGE ROLL-UP

Serge a set of roll-ups for a thoughtful gift or practical storage in your own home. Each one holds a 5-piece flatware place setting. (Fig. 2-11)

## SKILLS USED:

Serge-finished edges; serged seams.

## Materials needed for each roll-up:

◆ One 10″ by 20″ (25.5cm by 51cm) rectangle of heavy flannel or flannel specially treated for storing silver

◆ ⅔ yard (.6m) of ⅜″-wide (1cm) satin or grosgrain ribbon in a matching or contrasting color

◆ Matching or contrasting-color serger or all-purpose thread for serging; matching all-purpose thread for the sewing machine

*Fig. 2-11 Neatly finish the edges of these handy roll-ups using basic serging.*

## SERGER SETTING:

3- or 3/4-thread balanced stitch

*Stitch length:* Short

*Stitch width:* Medium to wide

*Needle:* Size 11/75

## How-tos:

Serge-seam using ¼″ (6mm) allowances, trimming if necessary.

1 From the right side, serge-finish one short end of the rectangle.

2 To form a pocket, fold 6″ (15cm) of the serge-finished end to the wrong side and pin it into position, matching the side cut edges.

*POSITION PINS PARALLEL TO AND ABOUT 1/2″ (1.3CM) INSIDE THE STITCHING LINE SO THEY WON'T INTERFERE WITH THE KNIVES OR A NEEDLE.*

3 Fold the ribbon in half crosswise. With the pocket side down, pin the ribbon fold to the right-hand edge, 4½" (11.5cm) from the fold. (Fig. 2-12)

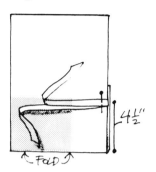

*Fig. 2-12 Position the folded ribbon so that it will be caught in the serging.*

4 With the ribbon on top, serge-finish the sides and upper edge, serge-seaming the sides of the pockets and catching the ribbon in the stitching. Be careful to remove the pin holding the ribbon before it reaches the knives. Knot and clip the thread chains.

5 From the pocket side, mark a line 2" (5cm) from the right-hand edge on the folded section. Mark four additional lines 1½" (4cm) from the first line and 1½" (4cm) apart. Top-stitch on these lines to form pockets for the silverware, being careful not to catch the ribbon in the stitching. (Fig. 2-13)

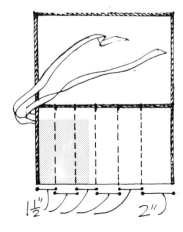

*Fig. 2-13 Sew pockets to hold a flatware place setting.*

*BACK-STITCH OR LOCK-STITCH AT THE ENDS OF THE STRAIGHT-STITCHING TO PREVENT IT FROM PULLING OUT.*

6 To use, insert a flatware place setting into the separate sections, leaving the left-hand one empty. Fold the flap down and begin rolling from the right-hand side. The empty section will wrap smoothly around the outside. Secure the roll-up by wrapping the ribbon around it and tying a bow.

*Fig. 2-14 Practice securing beginning stitches on this pretty little project.*

# EYELET-TRIMMED SACHET BAG

Use remnants of fabric, eyelet, and ribbon to create a sweet-smelling hang-up for a quick gift or for your own enjoyment. (Fig. 2-14)

### SKILLS USED:

Serged seams; securing beginning stitches.

3 From the right side, serge-finish the edges where the *Velcro* is attached, stitching through the upper edges of the sections positioned there.

**ADJUST THE DIFFERENTIAL FEED TO THE LOWEST SETTING AND HOLD THE FABRIC TAUT IN FRONT OF AND BEHIND THE PRESSER FOOT TO PREVENT THE NYLON FABRIC FROM SLIPPING WHILE SERGE-SEAMING.**

4 With right sides together, serge-seam the unfinished short edges together.

5 Pin the ends of the webbing strap to the right side of one rectangle, midway between the top edge and the center bottom of the bag. (Fig. 2-23)

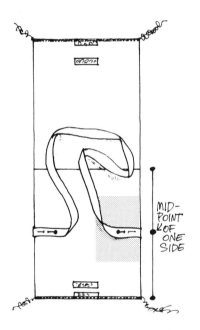

MID-POINT OF ONE SIDE

Fig. 2-23 *Pin the strap ends so that they will be caught in the serge-seaming.*

6 Fold the bag right sides together with the serge-finished edges matching. Serge-seam the sides, being sure to catch the strap ends but not the rest of the strap in the stitching. Reinforce the seam over the strap by straight-stitching along the serged needleline. Dab the thread chains with seam sealant and trim the excess when dry.

**WHEN SERGING OVER THE WEBBING, SERGE SLOWLY TO MAKE SURE YOU CATCH ALL LAYERS. TO AVOID HITTING A PIN, STOP SERGING WHEN THE PRESSER FOOT REACHES THE STRAP. REACH BETWEEN THE TWO FABRIC LAYERS AND REMOVE THE PIN, HOLDING ONTO THE STRAP. PLACE THE TOP FABRIC LAYER BACK INTO POSITION AND HOLD THE STRAP THROUGH IT AS YOU SERGE OVER IT.**

7 From the inside of the bag, refold one bottom corner to form a point, matching the serged seamlines in the center. Mark a line 2½" (6.5cm) from the point and perpendicular to the serging. Serge-seam on the line, trimming away the corner (as in Fig. 2-20). Repeat for the other corner.

8 Fold the top edge of the bag 1" (2.5cm) to the wrong side. From the wrong side, top-stitch through the center of the serge-finishing to secure the hem.

9 To permanently crease the bag edges, with wrong sides together, fold the bag from one bottom corner point evenly to the top edge. Edge-stitch close to the fold. Repeat for the other three corners. (Fig. 2-24)

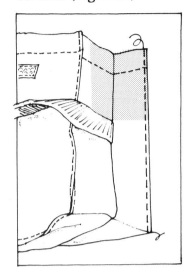

Fig. 2-24 *Edge-stitch the bag's folds to create crisp edges.*

10 Form the bag base by folding from corner to corner and edge-stitching on the folds.

11 To close the bag, seal the *Velcro* sections together on the opposite inside hem edges, then roll the hem allowance down twice and seal the remaining *Velcro* sections.

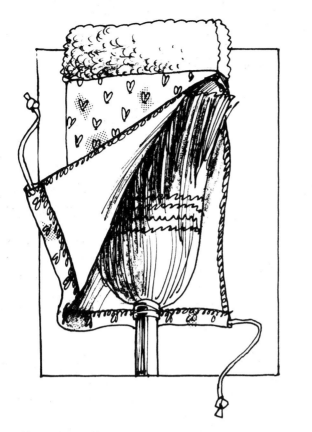

## CLEAN-SWEEP BROOM COVER

Slip this serged fleece-trimmed cover over a broom to dust and clean any hard-to-reach area. It's machine-washable, too! (Fig. 2-25)

### SKILLS USED:

Serged seam; serge-finished edges; serged, turned, and top-stitched hem casing; conventional seam with serge-finished allowances; serging fleece.

Fig. 2-25 The fleecy end of this tie-on broom cover grabs dirt quickly.

## Materials needed:

- One 20″ by 14″ (51cm by 35.5cm) rectangle of cotton/polyester print
- One 20″ by 5″ (51cm by 12.5cm ) rectangle of heavy polyester fleece
- 27″ (68.5cm) of ¼″ (6mm) cording or one 27″-long (68.5cm) shoelace
- Matching serger or all-purpose thread for serging; matching all-purpose thread for the sewing machine

### SERGER SETTINGS:

3- or 3/4-thread balanced stitch

**Stitch length:** Medium

**Stitch width:** Wide

**Needle:** Size 11/75

## How-tos:

Serge-seam using ¼″ (6mm) allowances, just skimming the fabric edge with the knives.

1 Pin one 20″ (51cm) side of the fabric and fleece rectangles, right sides together. With the fleece on the bottom, serge-seam the pinned edges. Finger-press the allowances toward the fabric.

ADJUST THE DIFFERENTIAL FEED TO APPROXIMATELY 1.75 OR LENGTHEN THE STITCH SLIGHTLY AND TIGHTEN THE NEEDLE TENSION TO PREVENT THE FLEECE FROM STRETCHING WHILE SERGE-SEAMING. IF THE FLEECE DOES STRETCH, TRIM IT TO EQUAL THE LENGTH OF THE FABRIC AFTER SERGE-SEAMING.

2 Adjust the serger back to normal settings. Serge-finish the other 20″ (51cm) edge of the fabric and the two fabric/fleece sides. Secure the ends by dabbing with seam sealant and clipping the thread chains when dry.

3 Press the serge-finished 20″ (51cm) fabric edge ¾″ (2cm) to the wrong side to form a hem casing. From the wrong side, top-stitch through the center of the serged stitching. (Fig. 2-26)

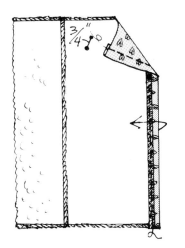

**Fig. 2-26** *Press up the hem casing and top-stitch down the middle of its serge-finished edge.*

4 To form the broom cover, fold the fabric/fleece rectangle crosswise, right sides together, with the hem casing on the bottom. Match the serge-finished side edges, the seamlines, and the fleece raw edges.

5 Serge-seam the fleece raw edges at the top of the cover. Secure the thread chain on the ends with seam sealant, then clip the excess thread chain when dry.

*TO PREVENT THE FLEECE FROM STRETCHING OUT OF SHAPE, LENGTHEN THE STITCH, ADJUST THE DIFFERENTIAL FEED TO ITS HIGHEST SETTING, OR EASE-PLUS BY GENTLY FEEDING THE FLEECE UNDER THE FRONT OF THE PRESSER FOOT FASTER THAN THE FEED DOGS WOULD NORMALLY TAKE IT IN. ALSO HOLD THE FABRIC AGAINST THE BACK OF THE PRESSER FOOT WITH YOUR LEFT INDEX FINGER, SLOWING DOWN ITS EXIT FROM UNDER THE FOOT. (SEE FIG. 1-17)*

6 Beginning at the fleece end, straight-stitch the side seam next to the serge-finishing. Sew ½" (1.3cm) past the fleece/fabric seam and back-stitch. (Fig. 2-27) Leave the rest of the side open.

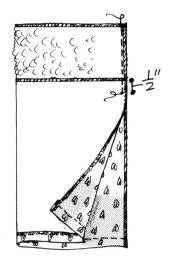

**Fig. 2-27** *Straight-stitch the side seam near the serge-finished edges.*

7 Thread the cording or shoe-lace through the casing and use it as a drawstring to hold the cover on the broom.

# 3 Specialty Seams & Edges

After you've learned the basic seams and edge finishes in Chapter 2, you can easily move on to specialty seams that involve more than one step and add durability or decorative detail to your project. Top-stitched seams are a simple example. (Fig. 3-1)

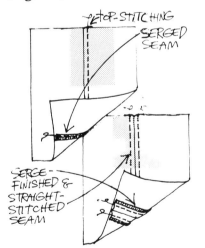

*Fig. 3-1  Top-stitch basic seams for durability or to add a decorative element.*

Other specialty seams, including lapped, French, and serged flat-felled, are also featured in this chapter's projects. For more information on specialty seams, see Chapters 9 and 10 in *ABCs of Serging*. Or see *Serged Garments in Minutes* for practical applications such as the neckline finishes in Chapter 4.

ALWAYS BEGIN BY TESTING A SPECIALTY SEAM ON SCRAPS OF THE PROJECT FABRIC TO CONFIRM THE FINAL EFFECT.

We've included a variety of curves and corners on both seams and edges to help improve your serging skills. In general:

- For the quickest and easiest results, serge off an outside corner and back onto the adjoining side. (See Fig. 1-20)

- For the easiest inside corners, always trim away the seam allowance (if there is one) before serging, then guide the knives along the fabric edge. Trimming an inside corner with the knives is more difficult.

- On curves and corner points, always serge **slowly**. Guide the fabric so that it feeds under the presser foot in a straight line. (See Figs. 1-21 and 1-22) For accuracy, watch the knives instead of the needle.

- When serge-seaming, check every few inches to be sure the underlayer is flat. This is especially important as you serge curves, because the knives could accidentally cut away too much fabric.

- To begin a neat opening when serge-seaming a project that will be turned and/or stuffed, first clear the stitch finger (see Fig. 1-23) and place the needle on the seamline. To end at the opposite side of the opening, stop with the needle and presser foot up, pull the fabric behind the needle, and serge off. (See Fig. 1-24)

- Overlap stitches to close an opening, finish serging in a circle, restart interrupted stitching, or repair uneven serging. First trim away any excess thread chain or irregular stitching. To begin overlapping, clear the stitch finger and position the needle on the seamline over the previous stitches about ½" from the end. Begin serging, being careful not to cut the original stitches. To end by overlapping, serge over the previous stitches about ½", again being careful not to cut them. Then raise the presser foot and needle, pull the fabric behind the needle, and serge off. (See Fig. 1-24) Secure the thread chain if necessary.

## TERRIFIC TAPESTRY VEST

Use buttonhole twist to decoratively serge-finish the lapped seam edges on this fashionable vest. Finish the fake welts and outer vest edges to match. (Fig. 3-2)

### SKILLS USED:

Lapped seams; serged seams; serge-finished edges.

## Materials needed:

♦ Loose-fitting vest pattern with welt pocket flaps, ⁵⁄₈″ seam allowances, and no darts (any buttonholes, buttons, facings, back ties, and pockets will be eliminated)

*Fig. 3-2 Serge a simple lap-seamed vest for maximum fashion mileage.*

♦ Medium- to heavy-weight fabric, such as tapestry, synthetic suede, or brocade with no definite right or wrong side, following the pattern yardage requirements (if the vest back calls for lining fabric, use matching fabric instead)

♦ Fusible interfacing, approximately 6″ by 7″ (15cm by 18cm)

♦ Several spools of matching or contrasting buttonhole twist for the upper looper

SPOOLS OF BUTTONHOLE TWIST USUALLY CONTAIN ONLY A SMALL AMOUNT OF YARDAGE, SO BE SURE YOU HAVE ENOUGH FOR TESTING, SERGE-FINISHING THE LAPPED SEAMS, AND SERGING AROUND THE OUTER EDGES OF THE VEST.

♦ Matching serger or all-purpose thread for the needle and lower looper; matching all-purpose thread for the sewing machine

♦ Glue stick

## Cutting directions:

■ Before cutting the vest, fit the pattern. Compare your bust, hip, and length measurements to those on the back of the pattern envelope or on the pattern-front piece and make any necessary alterations.

BECAUSE THE VEST IS LOOSE-FITTING, BODY MEASUREMENTS MAY BE APPROXIMATE.

■ Cut two vest fronts, one vest back, and two welt flaps from the fabric.

■ Cut fusible interfacing the same size as the welt flaps.

SERGER SETTINGS:

3-thread balanced stitch

**Stitch length:** Short

**Stitch width:** Medium to wide

**Needle:** Size 14/90

## How-tos:

Thread the buttonhole twist in the upper looper and test the stitch on fabric scraps, adjusting to a satin-length stitch. If the fabric edge ruffles or stretches, lengthen the stitch slightly and adjust the differential feed to a high setting. When serging the garment, leave several inches of thread chain as you begin and end each edge.

1  Fuse the interfacing to both welt flaps. Fold the flaps on the foldline, wrong sides together. With the flaps right side up, serge-finish the folds without trimming. With the same sides up, serge-seam the side edges, with the needle on the seamline and trimming the remainder of the seam allowances.

2  Smooth out the thread chain loops at the fold ends. Using a loop turner or a tapestry needle, pull the thread chain back through the stitching on the underside and clip the excess. (See Fig. 1-26)

3  Place the flaps right side down on the vest-front placement markings. The unfinished edge is above and the serged fold below. Straight-stitch using ⅝″ (1.5cm) seam allowances (from the cut edges), then trim the allowances to ¼″ (6mm). (Fig. 3-3)

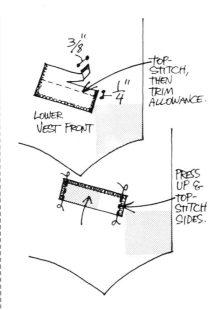

Fig. 3-3 Apply the welt flaps to the two vest-front sections.

4  Press the flaps up and top-stitch the side edges to the garment along the serging needleline.

5  From the right side of the two vest fronts and the wrong side of the vest back, serge-finish the shoulder and side seam allowances with the needle on the seamline, trimming approximately ⅜″ (1cm). (Fig. 3-4)

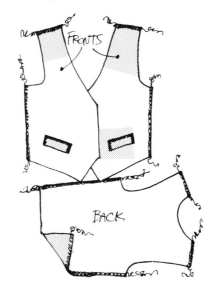

Fig. 3-4 Decoratively serge-finish the shoulder and side seams.

IF YOU RUN OUT OF BUTTONHOLE TWIST IN THE MIDDLE OF AN EDGE, REMOVE THE FABRIC FROM THE MACHINE AND CLIP AWAY ANY EXCESS THREAD TO NEATEN THE INTERRUPTED END. RETHREAD THE MACHINE AND TEST IT ON A SCRAP. THEN CLEAR THE STITCH FINGER (SEE FIG. 1-23) AND USE THE LAPPED SERGING TECHNIQUE ON PAGE 11 TO BEGIN AGAIN CLEANLY BEFORE COMPLETING THE EDGE.

6  Lap the front shoulder edges over the back shoulder edges, matching the needlelines. Glue-baste them in place using the glue stick and allow them to dry.

7  From the right side, top-stitch along the matched needlelines, through both layers. (Fig. 3-5)

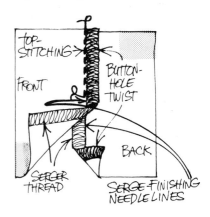

Fig. 3-5 Lap and glue-baste the seams before top-stitching the layers together, matching the needlelines.

8  With right sides up, serge-finish the armholes.

9  Lap the side seam of one vest front over the side seam of the vest back, matching the needlelines, and glue-baste. Top-stitch as in step 7. Repeat for the other side seam.

*10* Beginning and ending at one lower-front edge, serge-finish around the outer edges from the right side of the vest. If there are corner points, serge off the edge, pivot the fabric, and serge onto the adjoining edge. (Fig. 3-6)

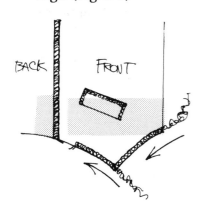

*Fig. 3-6 When serge-finishing the vest edges, serge off at each corner, pivot the fabric, and serge back on again.*

*11* Secure the corner thread chains by pulling the excess to the wrong side and following the instructions in step 2.

*Fig. 3-7 Choose a jacket pattern with dropped shoulder and a banded neckline for this speedy project.*

## EASY FRENCH-SEAMED JACKET

Serged French seaming professionally finishes this easy-to-make jacket, preventing unsightly show-through of the seam allowances on sheer fabric. It's also an excellent seam finish for a sleeve that will be worn rolled up. (Fig. 3-7)

**SKILLS USED:**

Serged seams; serged French seams; serged, turned, and top-stitched hems.

## Materials needed:

◆ Loose-fitting, unlined drop-shoulder jacket pattern with banded front, no pockets, and ⅝" (1.5cm) seam allowances

**SELECT A PATTERN WITH AS FLAT A SLEEVE CAP AS POSSIBLE FOR THE EASIEST FRENCH SEAMING.**

◆ Lightweight silky or sheer fabric, such as polyester woven, lace, or georgette, following the pattern yardage requirements

◆ Lightweight fusible interfacing for the band, if required

◆ Matching serger or all-purpose thread for serging; matching all-purpose thread for the sewing machine

## Cutting directions:

■ Before cutting the jacket, fit the pattern. Compare your bust, hip, jacket-length, and sleeve-length measurements to those on the back of the pattern envelope or on the pattern-front piece and make any necessary alterations.

**YOU MAY NEED TO PIN-FIT THE PATTERN TO DETERMINE THE CORRECT SLEEVE LENGTH.**

■ If the jacket sleeve is tapered, straighten and widen the sleeve pattern piece. Allow for a 1" (2.5cm) hem allowance. (Fig. 3-8)

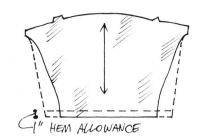

*Fig. 3-8 Straighten the sleeves, if necessary, for the easiest French seaming.*

■ Cut one jacket back, two jacket fronts, two sleeves, and two band sections.

■ Cut fusible interfacing for the two band sections.

**SERGER SETTINGS:**

3-thread balanced stitch

**Stitch length:** Medium

**Stitch width:** Narrow for French seaming; medium for serge-finishing and serge-seaming

**Needle:** Size 11/75

## How-tos:

When serging lightweight fabric, hold the fabric taut in front of and behind the presser foot and set the differential feed on the lowest setting to prevent puckering.

**TEST THE FRENCH SEAMING ON FABRIC SCRAPS. IF THE SERGING TENDS TO PULL OFF THE FABRIC, WIDEN THE STITCH SLIGHTLY.**

1 Fuse the interfacing to the band pieces following the pattern and manufacturer's instructions. Position two short ends right sides together and serge-seam, placing the needle on the seamline and trimming the remainder of the seam allowances. Fold the band in half lengthwise with the ends right sides together and serge-seam across them with the needle on the seamline and the excess seam allowance being trimmed. Turn the band right side out and press carefully.

2 From the right side, serge-finish the lower edges of the sleeves, jacket fronts, and jacket back.

3 Adjust to a narrow stitch for French seaming. Serge-seam the shoulder seams with wrong sides together. Do not serge with the needle on the seamline but trim about ¼" (6mm) as you serge, leaving a ⅛" (3mm) seam allowance and ¼" (6mm) for turning.

**WHEN NARROWING THE STITCH, YOU MAY NEED TO TIGHTEN THE LOOPER TENSIONS SO THAT THE THREAD OVERLOCKS ON THE FABRIC EDGE. IF YOU CANNOT TIGHTEN THE TENSIONS ENOUGH, ADJUST FOR A SLIGHTLY WIDER STITCH. TEST FIRST.**

4 Press the seam flat with the allowances to one side. Press again with the fabric right sides together and the serged seam between them. (Fig. 3-9)

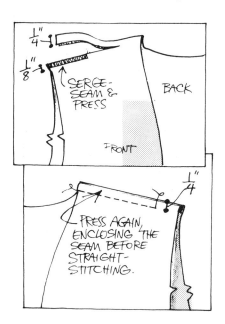

*Fig. 3-9 Use serged French seams to finish the jacket neatly.*

5 Straight-stitch ¼" (6mm) from the seam, enclosing the serged seam allowances. Press the bound seam allowance toward the back of the jacket.

6 With the wrong sides of the sleeves and jacket together and the markings matching, serge French seams, following steps 3 through 5. Press the bound seam allowances toward the sleeves. Press the sleeve hem allowances to the wrong side.

7 With seamlines matching and the side/sleeve sections wrong sides together, serge French seams, following steps 3 through 5. Press the bound seam allowances toward the jacket back.

**AS YOU SERGE OVER THE UNDERARM CURVE, PULL IT STRAIGHT AND STRETCH SLIGHTLY TO PREVENT THE SEAMS FROM POPPING WHEN THE JACKET IS WORN.**

8 Place the band and jacket right sides together, matching the center backs and aligning the lower band edges with the jacket hemline. Place pins horizontally, pointing toward the cut edges. Fold the jacket hem to the right side over the finished ends of the band. Beginning at one lower edge with the band on top, serge-seam the band to the jacket. Turn the hem to the wrong side at the corners and press the band seam allowance toward the jacket. From the right side, top-stitch ⅛" (3mm) from the seamline, securing the seam allowance underneath. (Fig. 3-10)

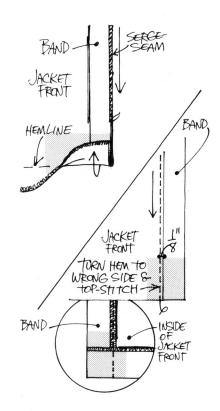

*Fig. 3-10 Fold the jacket hem to the right side over the band ends before serge-seaming. Top-stitch to hold the allowance in place.*

9 Turn and press all the hems to the wrong side. From the right side, top-stitch the sleeve hems, stitching through the serge-finishing on the underside. Top-stitch the jacket hem to match, but do not stitch through the band.

## NIFTY OVAL PLACEMATS

You'll never be short of placemats with these easy-to-serge favorites. They're washable, durable, and look great as well! (Fig. 3-11)

SKILLS USED:

Serged seams; serging curves.

### Materials needed:

◆ 1⅛ yard (1m) of 45"-wide (114cm) or ¾ yard (.7m) of 60"-wide (152cm) quilted or heavy, tightly woven fabric, such as denim, for six placemats

◆ 1⅛ yard (1m) of 45"-wide (114cm) or ¾ yard (.7m) of 60"-wide (152cm) matching or contrasting medium-weight fabric, such as percale, for the placemat backing

◆ Matching serger or all-purpose thread for serging; matching all-purpose thread for the sewing machine

*Fig. 3-11 Practice serging curved seams on these speedy placemats.*

### Cutting directions for each placemat:

■ Cut one 18" by 13" (46cm by 33cm) rectangle from both fabrics.

■ Round the corners of both rectangles, using a dinner plate as a guide.

SERGER SETTINGS:

3- or 3/4-thread balanced stitch

**Stitch length:** Medium

**Stitch width:** Medium

**Needle:** Size 14/90

### How-tos:

Serge-seam using ¼" (6mm) allowances, trimming if necessary. Repeat every step for each placemat.

*1* Place one placemat and one backing right sides together. Serge-seam around the placemat, leaving an opening for turning.

TO BEGIN AND END NEATLY, SEE PAGE 11 FOR HOW TO START AND STOP WHEN LEAVING AN OPENING. WHEN SERGING AROUND THE CURVES, WATCH THE KNIVES INSTEAD OF THE NEEDLE. SERGE SLOWLY TO GUIDE THE FABRIC ACCURATELY, HOLDING IT IN A STRAIGHT LINE IN FRONT OF THE PRESSER FOOT. IF THE STITCHING IS UNEVEN AROUND THE CURVES, NARROW THE STITCH SLIGHTLY AND SHORTEN THE STITCH LENGTH.

*2* Turn the placemat right side out through the opening and press carefully, folding the unserged seam allowances to the inside. Hand-stitch the opening closed.

*3* From the right side, top-stitch ¼" (6mm) from the seamline.

TOP-STITCH USING A TWIN-NEEDLE, A DECORATIVE MACHINE STITCH, OR A COMBINATION OF STITCHES FOR A DECORATIVE TOUCH. (FIG. 3-12)

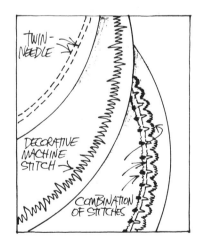

*Fig. 3-12 Be creative with your top-stitching to add variety.*

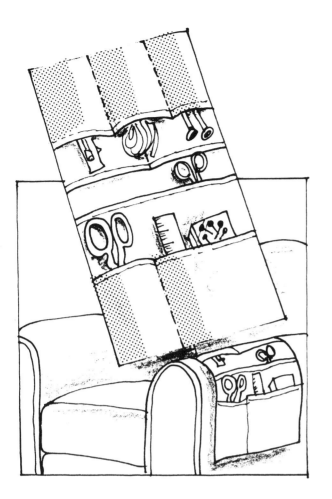

## FOLD-UP SEWING CADDY

Keep your sewing supplies and small projects at your fingertips. This handy organizer folds up to carry anywhere or hangs over the arm of your favorite chair. (Fig. 3-13)

### SKILLS USED:

Serged, turned, and top-stitched hems; serged seams; serging outside corners.

*Fig. 3-13 Learn to serge perfect outside corners as you make a useful sewing organizer.*

## Materials needed:

- ◆ ⅓ yard (.3m) of 45″-wide (114cm) heavy woven fabric, such as denim or canvas

- ◆ ⅓ yard (.3m) of the same fabric in a contrasting color or design

- ◆ Matching serger or all-purpose thread for serging; matching all-purpose thread for the sewing machine

- ◆ Seam sealant

## Cutting directions:

- From the first fabric, cut one 21″ by 12″ (53.5cm by 30.5cm) rectangle, two 7½″ by 12″ (19.5cm by 30.5cm) rectangles, and two 4½″ by 12″ (11.4cm by 30.5cm) rectangles.

- From the contrasting fabric, cut one 21″ by 12″ (53.5cm by 30.5cm) rectangle.

### SERGER SETTINGS:

3- or 3/4-thread balanced stitch

**Stitch length:** Medium

**Stitch width:** Wide

**Needle:** Size 14/90

## How-tos:

Serge-seam using ¼″ (6mm) allowances, just skimming the edges with the knives. When top-stitching the pockets, back-stitch or lock-stitch to secure the ends.

1 On each of the four small rectangles, serge-finish one long edge. Press ½″ (1.3cm) to the wrong side on each and top-stitch from the right side ⅜″ (1cm) from the fold to form hems.

2 Serge-finish the opposite long edge of the two smallest rectangles.

3 To find the center, press the largest fabric rectangle in half crosswise. Place the hemmed edge of both smallest rectangles ½" (1.3cm) on either side of the center crease and top-stitch them together through the serge-finished edges. Machine-baste the matching side edges together. Top-stitch down the center of one rectangle to form two pockets. (Fig. 3-14)

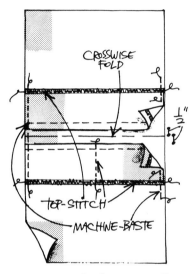

Fig. 3-14 *Apply the two smallest rectangles to the caddy base first.*

4 Place the other hemmed rectangles at either end of the larger rectangle, with cut edges matching and the hems toward the center. Machine-baste the cut edges together.

5 On one rectangle, top-stitch 4" (10cm) from each side to form three pockets. On the other rectangle, top-stitch 4" (10cm) from one side to form one large and one small pocket. (Fig. 3-15)

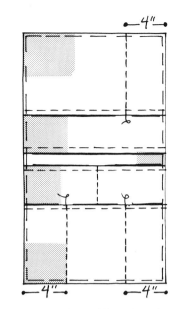

Fig. 3-15 *After adding the other hemmed rectangles, top-stitch to create additional pockets.*

6 Place the right sides of both large rectangles together. Serge-seam the cut edges, leaving an opening on one long edge for turning (see page 11 for how to start and stop neatly when leaving an opening). At the corners, simply serge off the edge at the corner, pivot the fabric, and serge onto the adjoining edge. Just skim the edge while serging. Secure the ends by dabbing a drop of seam sealant on the corners, then clip the excess thread when dry.

PREVENT DOG-EARED CORNERS BY ANGLING IN ABOUT 1/8" (3MM) FOR THE LAST THREE OR FOUR STITCHES BEFORE THE CORNER. ON THE ADJOINING EDGE, BEGIN ABOUT 1/8" (3MM) INSIDE THE STITCHING LINE AND ANGLE OUT ABOUT THE SAME DISTANCE. (FIG. 3-16)

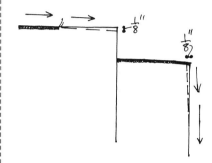

Fig. 3-16 *Give the corners the illusion of looking perfectly square by angling them in slightly at the point.*

7 Turn the caddy right side out and press carefully. Hand-stitch the opening closed.

BEFORE TURNING, PRESS THE SHORT-EDGE SEAM ALLOWANCES TOWARD THE CADDY, THEN PRESS THE OPPOSITE ALLOWANCES TOWARD THE CADDY, WRAPPING OVER THE FIRST ALLOWANCES AT THE CORNERS. WHEN YOU TURN THE CADDY RIGHT SIDE OUT, KEEP THE ALLOWANCES IN THIS POSITION SO THAT THE CORNERS WILL BE AS FLAT AS POSSIBLE.

# ROUND BALL PILLOW

Your serger quickly and neatly joins six curved seams to make a fun ball-shaped pillow. (Fig. 3-17)

### SKILLS USED:

Serged seams; serging curves.

## Materials needed:

- ◆ ²⁄₃ yard (.6m) of 45″-wide (114cm) closely woven fabric, such as corduroy or chintz
- ◆ One package of polyester fiberfill
- ◆ Matching serger or all-purpose thread
- ◆ Seam sealant

## Cutting directions:

Cut six pillow sections on the bias, following the pattern grid. (Fig. 3-18)

### SERGER SETTINGS:

3- or 3/4-thread balanced stitch

**Stitch length:** Medium

**Stitch width:** Wide

**Needle:** Size 11/75 for chintz; size 14/90 for heavier fabric

*Fig. 3-17  This round pillow is an interesting decorative accent and can also double as a toddler's toy.*

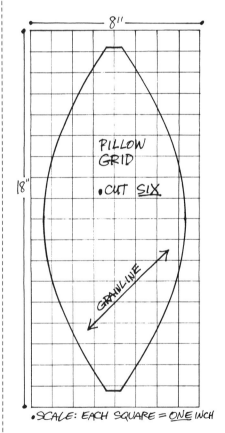

*Fig. 3-18  Cut out the pillow sections on the bias.*

## How-tos:

Serge-seam using ¼″ (6mm) allowances, just skimming the edges with the knives.

1 Join three pillow sections, right sides together, by serge-seaming the sides from point to point and guiding the curved edges as described on page 10. Repeat for the other three sections. (Fig. 3-19)

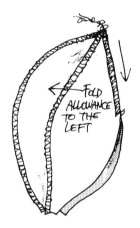

*Fig. 3-19  Serge-seam three sections together on both halves of the pillow.*

**TO SEAM THREE SECTIONS SMOOTHLY, SERGE-SEAM TWO SECTIONS FIRST.  THEN FOLD THE SERGED SEAM ALLOWANCE TO THE LEFT AND, WITH THE SEAMED SECTION ON TOP, SERGE-SEAM THE THIRD SECTION.**

2 With right sides together and matching the raw edges, serge-seam the two sectioned pieces together, leaving an opening on one edge for turning and stuffing. See page 11 for how to start and stop neatly when leaving an opening. (Fig. 3-20)

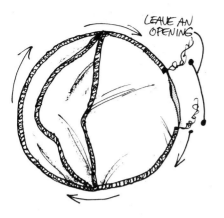

Fig. 3-20 *Join the two pillow halves right sides together.*

3  Dab a drop of seam sealant where the seams are joined. When dry, turn the pillow right side out.

4  Stuff the pillow firmly with fiberfill. Hand-stitch the opening closed.

# LACY REVERSIBLE HANKY

Show off your serging skills by sporting a round lace-edged hanky in your jacket pocket. Fold the hanky with the opposite side out to display a contrasting color. (Fig. 3-21)

### SKILLS USED:

Serging in a circle; serged seam.

## Materials needed:

◆ ⅓ yard (.3m) of lightweight woven fabric, such as batiste

◆ ⅓ yard (.3m) of the same fabric in a contrasting color

◆ 1¼ yard (1.1m) of ¾"-wide (2cm) ruffled lace

## Cutting directions:

Cut two 10½"-diameter (27cm) circles, using a lid or dinner plate as a guide.

### SERGER SETTINGS:

3-thread balanced stitch

**Stitch length:** Medium

**Stitch width:** Medium

**Needle:** Size 11/75

## How-tos:

Serge-seam using ¼"(6mm) allowances, trimming if necessary.

1  Fold one end of the lace ½" (1.3cm) to the wrong side. Position the matched edges of the lace and one circle under the presser foot with right sides together and the lace on top. Lowering the needle into the seamline, serge-seam, easing the lace to the circle. To finish, fold the lace end under ½" (1.3cm) and lap it ½" (1.3cm) over the beginning end. (Fig. 3-22)

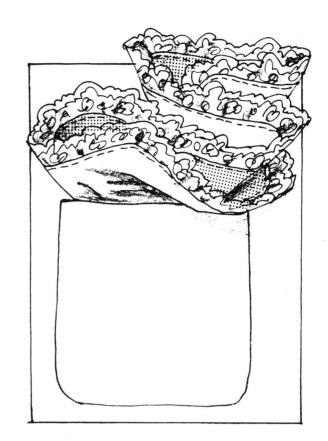

Fig. 3-21 *Learn how to apply lace to a circle in this quick project.*

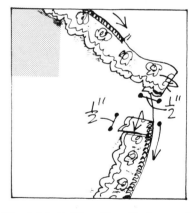

Fig. 3-22 *Fold and lap the lace ends as you serge-seam the lace to the circle.*

SERGE SLOWLY TO GUIDE THE STITCHING ACCURATELY. AS YOU MOVE THE CURVE TO THE RIGHT IN FRONT OF THE FOOT, YOU MAY HAVE TO RAISE THE FOOT OCCASIONALLY TO EASE THE FABRIC UNDERNEATH IT. HOLD THE FABRIC TAUT UNDERNEATH THE LACE AND ADJUST THE DIFFERENTIAL FEED TO THE LOWEST SETTING.

2 Steam above the lace and finger-press the lace toward the center of the hanky.

3 Place the two circles right sides together. With the lace-finished circle up, serge-seam over the previous stitching, leaving an opening for turning. (See page 11 for techniques to start and stop evenly.)

4 Turn the hanky right side out and press carefully, pulling the lace away from the hanky and folding the allowances inside the opening. From the right side, top-stitch close to the seam to secure the allowance and close the opening. (Fig. 3-23)

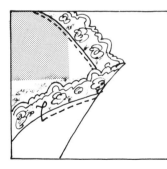

*Fig. 3-23 With the lace extending away from the hanky, top-stitch through both circular layers, catching the allowance between them.*

# DENIM LAUNDRY BAG

Practice a serged flat-felled seam on the front of a handy drawstring laundry bag. (Fig. 3-24)

### SKILLS USED:

Serged, turned, and top-stitched hem; serge-finished edges; mock flat-felled seam; serged seam.

*Fig. 3-24 You'll use several different serging skills when you make this practical yet decorative bag.*

## Materials needed:

◆ ³/₄ yard (.7m) of 45"-wide (114cm) heavy woven fabric, such as denim (Pretreat denim to soften the fabric and help make the construction easier.)

◆ 1¹/₃ yard (1.2m) of heavy cording

◆ Matching or contrasting serger or all-purpose thread for serging; matching or contrasting all-purpose thread for the sewing machine

◆ Seam sealant

## Cutting directions:

- Cut one 45" by 25" (114cm by 63.5cm) rectangle.
- Cut one 45" by 1½" (114cm by 4cm) strip for the casing.

**SERGER SETTINGS:**

3-thread balanced stitch

**Stitch length:** Medium

**Stitch width:** Wide

**Needle:** Size 14/90

## How-tos:

Serge-seam using ¼"(6mm) allowances, just skimming the edges with the knives.

1 Serge-finish one long edge of the large rectangle and both long edges of the strip.

2 On the large rectangle, press the serge-finished edge 1" (2.5cm) to the wrong side. Top-stitch at ⅞" (2.25cm) to secure the hem.

3 Fold ¾" (2cm) to the wrong side on one end of the strip. With both right sides up, place the strip on the larger rectangle ¾" (2cm) from the upper edge and 1½" (4cm) from one side edge. End the casing 1½" (4cm) from the opposite side edge, folding ¾" (2cm) to the wrong side and trimming the excess.

4 Top-stitch the strip through the center of both rows of serge-finishing to form a casing. (Fig. 3-25)

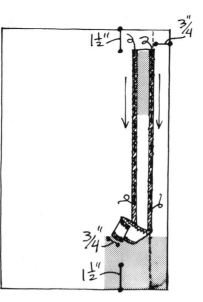

*Fig. 3-25 Top-stitch the strip to the rectangle for the drawstring casing.*

**IT'S ALWAYS EASIEST TO COMPLETE AS MANY STEPS AS POSSIBLE WHILE THE PROJECT IS STILL FLAT.**

5 Fold the rectangle crosswise with right sides together and the hem at the top. Matching the seamlines, straight-stitch the side using a ⅝" (1.5cm) seam allowance.

6 Serge-finish the allowances together, trimming slightly as you serge. Press the allowances to one side. Dab seam sealant on the ends to secure them. (Fig. 3-26)

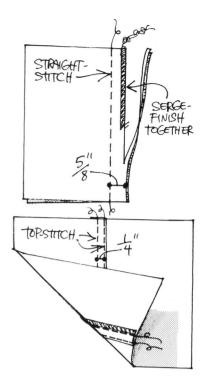

*Fig. 3-26 Press the serge-finished allowances to the side before top-stitching through them.*

7 From the right side, top-stitch through all layers just next to the seamline and again ¼" (6mm) away.

8 Refold the bag right sides together to center the seam. Serge-seam the lower edge. Dab seam sealant on the ends and trim the excess thread chain when dry. (Fig. 3-27)

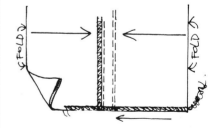

*Fig. 3-27 Center the serged flat-felled seam before serge-seaming the bag bottom.*

9 Turn the bag right side out. Thread the cording through the casing and knot both ends.

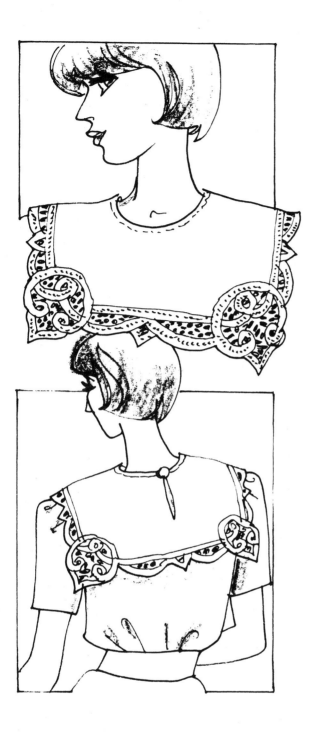

## BATTENBURG LACE COLLAR

Made from a Battenburg placemat, this easy collar has the appearance of an elaborate hand-worked treasure. (Fig. 3-28)

*Fig. 3-28 Even though several different serging skills are used, you can easily make this distinctive collar.*

### SKILLS USED:

Serge-finishing a slit; serged seams; securing beginning stitches; serging curves; serged, turned, and top-stitched edges; thread-chain button loop.

### Materials needed:

◆ One Battenburg lace placemat (available in linen or department stores)

◆ Jewel-neck top pattern with a back-slit opening

◆ One small matching ball button

◆ Matching or contrasting serger or all-purpose thread for serging; matching all-purpose thread for the sewing machine

### Cutting directions:

■ Press the placemat in half crosswise to establish the front and back of the collar.

■ Cut one collar front using the press-mark as the top edge of the fabric.

■ Cut one collar back and the slit opening with the shoulder edges directly opposite the front.

■ Trim the shoulder and neckline seam allowances to ¼" (6mm).

### SERGER SETTINGS:

3-thread balanced stitch

**Stitch length:** Medium

**Stitch width:** Narrow

**Needle:** Size 11/75

### How-tos:

1 To finish the slit, serge one edge from the right side, stopping when the knives are about ½" (1.3cm) from the end of the slit with the needle in the down position.

2 Raise the presser foot and swing the fabric in front of the foot toward your left so that the slit forms a straight line. Lower the foot and continue serging. (Fig. 3-29)

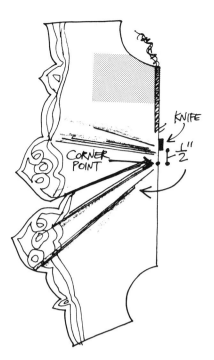

Fig. 3-29 Stop before the knives reach the corner point and swing the opposite side of the slit around so the entire edge forms a straight line.

YOU WON'T BE TRIMMING THE FABRIC AS YOU SERGE—JUST GUIDE THE SLIT EDGE NEXT TO THE KNIFE, SERGING SLOWLY AT THE SLIT POINT AND BEING SURE TO CATCH THE NEEDLE IN THE FABRIC THERE. (IF YOU HAVE TROUBLE, USE YOUR FINGER TO PUSH THE FABRIC TOWARD THE NEEDLE AT THE POINT.) YOU'LL NOTICE THAT WHEN THE SLIT EDGE IS PULLED INTO A STRAIGHT LINE, A TUCK OR TUCKS WILL FORM IN THE FABRIC, EXTENDING FROM THE CORNER POINT. WHEN YOU BRING THE EDGE BACK TO ITS ORIGINAL ANGLE, THE TUCKS WILL DISAPPEAR.

3 Press the serge-finished slit edge to the wrong side along the stitching needleline. Edge-stitch around the slit opening, catching the turned-back allowance. Stitch very close to the edge at the corner point because the allowance will narrow there as it stretches around the bottom of the slit. (Fig. 3-30)

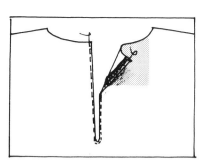

Fig. 3-30 Press and edge-stitch the serge-finished edge to the wrong side.

4 With right sides together and beginning at the lace edges, serge-seam the shoulders. To neatly secure the beginning stitches, serge several inches of thread chain and then serge two stitches onto the lace edge. With the needle in the fabric, raise the presser foot and wrap the thread chain toward the front, under the presser foot. (See Fig. 2-16) Serge over the chain to secure it and let the knives trim the excess tail after 1" (2.5cm). Press the seam allowances toward the collar back.

PULL THE THREAD CHAIN FIRMLY TOWARD THE FRONT UNDER THE PRESSER FOOT WHEN BEGINNING SO THAT AN EXCESS LOOP OF THREAD WILL NOT BE EXPOSED ON THE EDGE OF THE FABRIC.

5 Serge-finish the curved neckline edge beginning at the right-back slit edge. Serge slowly to guide the fabric accurately around the curves, moving the fabric into a straight line in front of the presser foot. Serge off the opposite edge, leaving several inches of thread chain.

6 Carefully press the neckline edge ³/₈" (1cm) to the wrong side. Top-stitch ¹/₄" (6mm) from the fold to secure it. At the left-back slit edge, thread the excess thread chain through a large needle and hand-sew the chain at the upper corner to form a button loop. Knot securely and trim the excess. (Fig. 3-31)

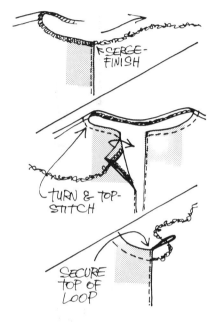

Fig. 3-31 Bring the excess thread chain around to form a button loop on the left side of the slit.

7 At the right-back slit edge, knot the chain securely and clip the excess. Sew the button at the corner.

# 4 Gathering, Easing, & Shirring

You can use your serger to quickly gather or ease an edge or fold with basic stitching and one of several possible techniques. A high differential-feed setting, tightened needle tension, and a longer stitch all can help gather the fabric as it is serged.

WHEN YOU CHANGE ANY OF THE MACHINE'S SETTINGS FOR GATHERING, ALWAYS REMEMBER TO ADJUST THEM BACK TO NORMAL FOR REGULAR BALANCED SERGING.

Pulling on the needle thread after serging with loosened needle-thread tension can gather or ease fabric. Because the needle thread can break when pulled too hard, this method is best for short sections or for a little additional gathering on a previously gathered edge.

Clear elastic can also be used for serge-gathering by stretching it over the fabric edge and serging through both the elastic and fabric. The fabric gathers up when the elastic is released. See the Gathered Three-tiered Skirt on page 53 for all the details.

Another technique that works well on any weight fabric and for longer sections involves serging over a filler cord and pulling it to gather or ease:

1 Thread filler cord (such as pearl cotton or cotton crochet thread) under the back and over the front of the presser foot, carefully guiding it between the needle and the knives. (Fig. 4-1)

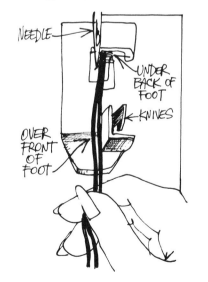

Fig. 4-1 *Position one or more strands of filler cord carefully so that you won't cut it or stitch into it as you serge.*

IF YOUR SERGER MODEL HAS A FOOT WITH A BUILT-IN CORDING OR TAPE GUIDE OR AN OPTIONAL ONE SPECIALLY DESIGNED FOR FEEDING BEADING OR RIBBON, USE IT TO GUIDE THE FILLER CORD ACCURATELY. (FIG. 4-2)

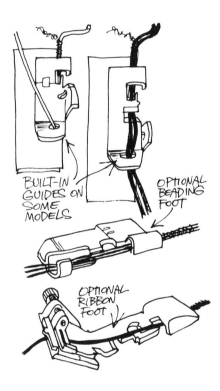

Fig. 4-2 *Take advantage of a special foot, if one is available.*

2 Using a wide, medium-length balanced 3-thread stitch, serge slowly over several inches of the filler cord, being careful not to stitch into it or cut it with the knives.

OR USE THE 3/4-THREAD STITCH, AS ILLUSTRATED IN FIG. 11-11 IN ABCS OF SERGING, GUIDING THE FILLER CORD BETWEEN THE TWO NEEDLES FOR MORE ACCURACY.

3 Insert the fabric edge or fold under the presser foot and filler cord and continue serging the area to be gathered.

4 At the end of the fabric, raise the needle and presser foot, pull the filler-cord end under the foot and gently pull both the fabric and cord behind the needle, then chain off. (See Fig. 1-24)

5 On a short edge, where the cord could pull out, secure one end around a pin or by straight-stitching back and forth across it, and pull the opposite end to gather the fabric. On a longer edge, pull the filler cord from both ends.

6 After gathering the desired amount, secure the remaining filler-cord end (or both ends if neither are secured).

Use the same filler-cord technique over elastic cording or narrow elastic for serge-shirring, creating built-in stretch. Serge over elastic on several parallel folds for a smocked effect.

FOR MORE SPECIFICS ON GATHERING, EASING, AND SHIRRING TECHNIQUES, SEE CHAPTER 11 IN ABCS OF SERGING OR, FOR GARMENT-RELATED APPLICATIONS, SEE CHAPTER 6 IN SERGED GARMENTS IN MINUTES.

# CLASSIC BUTTON-FRONT BLOUSE

Integrate speedy serging techniques into the conventional pattern instructions when making a basic blouse. (Fig. 4-3)

SKILLS USED:

Serged seams; serge-finished edges; serging a sleeve placket; serge-gathering; serge-easing; serged, turned, and top-stitched hem.

## Materials needed:

◆ Loose-fitting basic blouse pattern with one-piece collar and cuffs, cut-on facing, flat sleeve cap, and sleeves gathered or pleated at the lower edge

Fig. 4-3 Your serger speeds up blouse construction while finishing the seams and edges beautifully.

SELECT THE PATTERN SIZE BY COMPARING YOUR BUST MEASUREMENT TO THOSE LISTED ON THE BACK OF THE PATTERN ENVELOPE.

◆ Light- or medium-weight woven fabric, such as cotton-polyester, polyester, or rayon, following the pattern yardage requirements

◆ Fusible interfacing, following the pattern yardage requirements

◆ Buttons

◆ Matching serger or all-purpose thread for serging; matching all-purpose thread for the sewing machine

◆ Seam sealant

## Cutting directions:

- Pin-fit the pattern to determine the correct sleeve length by pinning the bodice, sleeve, and cuff pattern pieces together as they will be sewn. Make any necessary length adjustments on the sleeve pattern shorten/lengthen line.

*BEND YOUR ARM SLIGHTLY WHEN FITTING THE PATTERN. ALLOW SOME EXTRA LENGTH FOR THE SLEEVE TO BLOUSE AND FOR SHOULDER PADS, IF THEY WILL BE USED.*

- Cut two blouse fronts, one blouse back, two sleeves, two cuffs, and one collar. Eliminate any pockets that are included on the pattern.

- Cut fusible interfacing for the facings, collar, and cuffs

### SERGER SETTINGS:

3- or 3/4-thread balanced stitch

**Stitch length:** Medium

**Stitch width:** Wide

**Needle:** Size 11/75

## How-tos:

Serge-seam with the left needle on the ⅝" (1.5cm) seamline, trimming the excess seam allowance as you serge.

1 With wrong sides together, fuse the interfacing to the facings, collar, and cuffs, following the manufacturer's instructions.

2 With right sides together, serge-seam the shoulders and serge-finish the outer facing edges. Press the shoulder seam allowances toward the back. (Fig. 4-4)

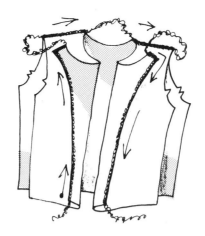

Fig. 4-4 *Serge continuously and clip the center of the joined thread chains when finished.*

*CONTINUOUSLY SERGE AS MANY EDGES OR SEAMS AS YOU CAN TO SAVE TIME. LEAVE ABOUT 4" (10.5CM) OF THREAD CHAIN BETWEEN EACH SEAM AND EDGE AND CLIP THE THREAD CHAINS LATER TO SEPARATE THE SECTIONS. YOU SAVE TIME AND HAVE AN EASIER TIME HANDLING THE FABRIC WHEN YOU SERGE EDGES AND SEAMS WHILE THEY ARE FLAT.*

3 Serge-seam the collar and cuff side seams and turn right side out. Press, rolling the seams slightly to the underside of the collar and cuffs.

4 Place the underside of the collar on the right side of the garment, matching the center backs and the notches or dots. Machine-baste the collar to the garment.

5 Fold the facings to the right side of the garment along the foldlines, sandwiching the collar between the facings and the garment. Serge-seam the neckline edge. Dab seam sealant on the ends and clip the excess thread chain when dry. (Fig. 4-5)

Fig. 4-5 *Fold the facings back over the right side of the garment and collar before serge-seaming the neckline edge.*

6 Cut a 3" (7.5cm) slit on both marked sleeve plackets. Adjust the serger to a medium-length, medium-width stitch and serge-finish both slits from the right side of the fabric. (See page 46, steps 1 and 2, for instructions on how to finish the slit neatly.)

*MAKE SURE TO CATCH THE POINT OF THE SLIT AS YOU SERGE OVER IT BY PUSHING THE FABRIC TOWARD THE NEEDLE, KEEPING THE NEEDLE IN THE FABRIC, EVEN THOUGH THE LOOPS MAY BE SLIGHTLY OFF THE EDGE. (FIG. 4-6)*

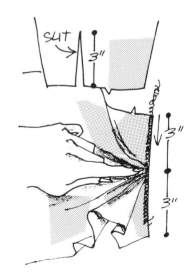

Fig. 4-6 *To catch the point of the slit in the serging, push it toward the needle with your index finger.*

7 Fold the slit opening right sides together, matching the serged edges. Straight-stitch a 1"-long (2.5cm) dart at the end of the slit. Begin just before the end of the serging along the inside edge of the stitches and taper to a point. Knot the thread ends and clip the excess. (Fig. 4-7)

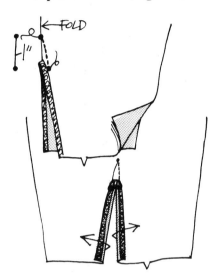

Fig. 4-7 *Sew a dart at the top of the slit before pressing the serge-finished edges to the wrong side.*

8 Press the serge-finished edges to the wrong side, parallel to the dart edges.

9 Adjust the serger for a wide stitch. Serge-seam the sleeve underarms and the blouse sides. Press the seam allowances toward the back of the blouse and the sleeves. Serge-finish the lower edge of the blouse.

10 Adjust the differential feed to its highest setting. If your serger does not have differential feed, lengthen the stitch and tighten the needle tension. Test the amount of serge-gathering on a scrap of the project fabric, allowing the fabric to feed freely into the machine. Adjust the amount of gathering by varying the differential-feed setting, stitch length, or needle tension. A higher setting, longer stitch, and tighter tension will gather more, while a lower setting, shorter stitch, or looser tension all produce fewer gathers.

*TO CREATE MORE GATHERS AFTER MAKING THE MAXIMUM ADJUSTMENTS, EASE-PLUS BY GENTLY FORCE-FEEDING THE FABRIC UNDER THE FRONT OF THE PRESSER FOOT AND HOLDING IT BACK AS IT EXITS OUT THE BACK. (SEE FIG. 1-17)*

11 After testing, serge-gather the lower edge of both sleeves with the needle on the seamline to fit the length of the finished cuffs. (Even if your pattern specifies pleats, gathers can be substituted.)

12 On both sleeves, place the cuff and sleeve right sides together and wrap the placket edges toward the underside of the cuff. Adjust the gathers by sliding the fabric along the serged needleline. (Fig. 4-8)

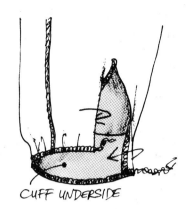

CUFF UNDERSIDE

Fig. 4-8 *Wrap the slit edges around the cuff ends so that they will turn to the underside when the blouse is right side out.*

13 Return to a normal setting and, with the cuffs on top, serge-seam the cuffs to the sleeves through all layers and secure the ends with seam sealant. Turn the cuffs right side out and the placket allowances will automatically wrap to the inside.

14 Pin the sleeves to the garment, with right sides together and markings matching. Straight-stitch with the garment on the top and the sleeves underneath, allowing the sewing machine feed dogs to ease the sleeves into the garment.

15 Adjust the differential feed to a 1.5 or slight positive setting. On both sleeves, serge-finish the seam allowances together, with the garment on top and trimming about 1/8" (3mm), overlapping the beginning serging about 1/2" (1.3cm). Clip the excess thread chain. Press the seam allowances only.

*SERGE SLOWLY, KEEPING THE SEAM ALLOWANCES FLAT ON THE UNDERSIDE AND BEING CAREFUL NOT TO CATCH THE SLEEVES IN THE SERGING.*

You'll use only basic serged seams and edges to make this simple tote and the other projects featured in Chapter 2.

This charming ruffled bow pillow is one of the featured projects in Chapter 4, which shows you how to quickly gather using your serger.

Flatlock over narrow ribbon
to embellish a pretty teacup
pincushion. All the details
are in Chapter 7.

Decorative flatlocked seams are featured on this sporty polar-fleece pullover from Chapter 7.

Specialty seams and edges are featured in the projects in Chapter 3. Here, we showcase a fashionable vest constructed with lapped seams.

Add a unique accent to rolled-edge napkins by weaving
a contrasting strip through buttonholes. See Chapter 6
for directions and other rolled-edge projects.

Put your serging skills to work on the
decorative serging projects featured in
Chapter 8. This simple roll-up knit-
ting-needle case, shown both open
and fastened, is finished with pearl
cotton.

From a terry bath mitt and headband to an interlock nightshirt and *Lycra* swimsuit, the projects featured in Chapter 5 are made using a variety of knit fabrics.

**16** Fold the facings to the right side of the blouse at the lower edge. Straight-stitch across the lower edges even with the blouse hemline. Trim the allowance to ¼" (6mm) in the facing area only.

**17** Fold the facings right side out and press the hem allowance to the wrong side. Straight-stitch the hem in place through the serge-finished edge.

**18** Carefully press and pin the facings in place at the shoulder line. From the right side, stitch-in-the-ditch of the shoulder seamlines, catching and securing the facing on the wrong side.

**19** Complete the garment by sewing buttons and buttonholes following the pattern instructions.

## GATHERED MULTI-TIERED SKIRT

Use clear elastic to easily gather the tiers of this fashion-right skirt. Clear elastic won't lose its stretch after you've serged through it. (Fig. 4-9)

### SKILLS USED:

Serged seams; elastic gathering; serged, turned, and top-stitched hem; serged pull-on elasticized waistband.

### *Materials needed:*

◆ Skirt pattern with two or more tiers and a cut-on elastic waistband casing

◆ Woven or knit fabric, following the pattern yardage requirements

FOR A FASHIONABLE EFFECT, USE A DIFFERENT COORDINATING FABRIC IN EACH TIER. CHECK THE PATTERN ENVELOPE TO SEE IF IT LISTS YARDAGE REQUIREMENTS FOR EACH TIER.

◆ ⅜"-wide (1cm) clear elastic, the length of the lower edge of each tier you'll be gathering fabric to, plus ½ yard (.5cm) (Fig. 4-10)

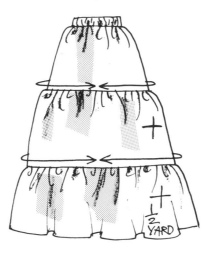

*Fig. 4-10 Measure the lower edge of the tiers (with the exception of the bottom one) and add 1/2 yard to determine the amount of elastic needed.*

*Fig. 4-9 Speedy elastic-gathering and serge-seaming make quick work of a multi-tiered skirt.*

◆ 1¼"-wide (3cm) sport or sew-through elastic, the length of the waistline measurement

FOR MORE SPECIFIC ELASTIC INFORMATION, SEE THE CHART ON PAGE 81 OF *SERGED GARMENTS IN MINUTES.*

◆ Matching serger or all-purpose thread for serging; matching all-purpose thread for the sewing machine

◆ Water-soluble marker

## Cutting directions:

- Adjust the waistline allowance for 1¼″-wide (3cm) elastic by cutting the casing 2½″ (6.5cm) wide, straight up from the waistline. Check to be sure the waistline circumference is large enough to pull over your hips. If more width is needed, add to the upper-tier seam allowances.

- Cut the tiers according to the pattern instructions, leaving only a ¼″ (6mm) hem allowance at the lower edge of the bottom tier.

**SERGER SETTINGS:**

3- or 3/4 thread balanced stitch

**Stitch length:** Medium

**Stitch width:** Wide

**Needle:** Size 11/75

## How-tos:

Serge-seam with the needle on the seamline (the left needle of a 3/4-thread machine), trimming the excess seam allowance if ⅝″ (1.5cm) allowances were used on the pattern.

1 Serge-seam each tier into a circle.

2 Stretch the clear elastic several times to prevent any additional stretching out after it is serged.

3 Measure the lower edge of the first skirt tier. Mark this measurement on the clear elastic and then quartermark it, using the marker. Do not cut the elastic. Also quartermark the wrong-side upper edge of the second skirt tier using the marker (or another visible marker, such as chalk, if the fabric is dark). For 2″ (5cm) on both sides of one mark, pretrim the seam allowance to ¼″ (6mm), cutting away ⅜″ (1cm). (Fig. 4-11)

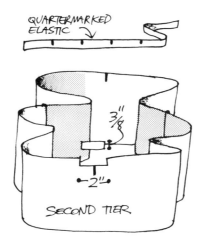

**Fig. 4-11** *Quartermark the elastic and the tier, then cut out a section to begin serging exactly on the seamline.*

4 Place the end of the elastic on the marking where the allowance has been trimmed away. Adjust to a long stitch and serge several stitches through the elastic and fabric. Then stretch the elastic to meet the quartermarks on the skirt, continuing to serge to the beginning end of the elastic. Lap the elastic ends ½″ (1.3cm). Raise the presser foot, pull the elastic and fabric behind the needle, and chain off. Trim off the remaining unstitched elastic for use on the other tiers. (Fig. 4-12)

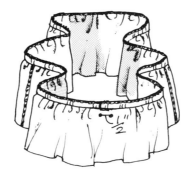

**Fig. 4-12** *Serge-seam the elastic to the top of the tier, matching quartermarks and lapping the ends.*

*TO MINIMIZE THE STRETCH OF THE ELASTIC, ADJUST THE DIFFERENTIAL FEED TO THE HIGHEST SETTING TO HELP EASE THE SKIRT'S FULLNESS TO THE ELASTIC.*

5 Position the upper edge of the second tier right sides together, against the lower edge of the first tier, matching the side seams. Readjust to a medium-length stitch and serge-seam the tiers together, overlapping the stitching for ½″ (1.3cm) before serging off the fabric.

6 Repeat the elastic application and serge-seaming for each additional skirt tier.

7 Serge-finish the lower edge of the skirt. Press the serged edge to the wrong side along the needleline. From the right side, top-stitch close to the fold.

8 Measure the wider elastic comfortably around your waist and add ½″ (1.3cm) for lapping, then trim. Sew the elastic into a circle by overlapping the ends and zigzagging them together.

9 Using pins (to help control the heavier elastic), quartermark both the elastic and the waistline edge. Readjust to a long stitch. With the elastic on top and matching the quartermarks, serge-seam the elastic to the wrong side of the waistline edge, stretching the elastic to fit the opening. Overlap the serging about ½″ (1.3cm) before serging off the edge.

*ADJUST THE DIFFERENTIAL FEED TO THE HIGHEST SETTING TO HELP EASE THE FABRIC TO THE ELASTIC AND PREVENT THE ELASTIC FROM STRETCHING OUT.*

10 Turn the elastic to the wrong side, enclosing it. From the wrong side, straight-stitch through the serged edge, catching all layers. Use a long stitch and stretch as you sew. (Fig. 4-13)

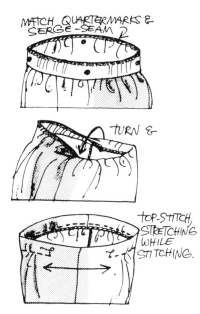

MATCH QUARTERMARKS & SERGE-SEAM

TURN &

TOP-STITCH, STRETCHING WHILE STITCHING.

*Fig. 4-13  Try this easy serged and turned waistband instead of enclosing the elastic in a casing.*

11 From the right side, stitch-in-the-ditch of the side seamlines to prevent the elastic from rolling in the casing

*INSTEAD OF STITCHING-IN-THE-DITCH, YOU MAY CHOOSE TO TOP-STITCH ONE OR MORE ADDITIONAL ROWS THROUGH THE WAISTBAND FROM THE RIGHT SIDE, STRETCHING AS YOU SEW.*

12 From the wrong side, steam well to shrink the elastic back to its original length, being careful not to touch the fabric with the iron.

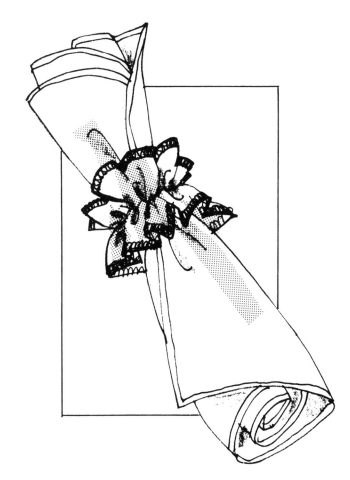

# SERGE-GATHERED NAPKIN RINGS

Quickly serge a last-minute set of gathered napkin rings as a thoughtful gift or to complement a special meal. (Fig. 4-14)

### SKILLS USED:

Serge-finished edges; filler-cord gathering.

## Materials needed:

◆ ⅓ yard (.3m) of 45"-wide (114cm) woven fabric, for six rings

◆ ½ yard (.5m) of paper-backed fusible web

◆ 3 yards (2.75m) of filler-cord, such as pearl cotton or cotton crochet thread

◆ Matching serger or all-purpose thread for serging; matching all-purpose thread for the sewing machine

*Fig. 4-14  They're simply fused, serge-finished, and gathered.*

## Cutting directions:

■ Fuse the paper-backed web to the wrong side of one 45" by 6" (114cm by 15cm) half of the fabric, following the manu-facturer's instructions. Remove the paper backing, fold the wrong side of the unfused fabric over the exposed web and fuse it in place, sand-wiching the web in between.

■ Cut the fused fabric into six 3" by 12" (7.5cm by 30.5cm) strips.

### SERGER SETTINGS:

3- or 3/4-thread balanced stitch

**Stitch length:** Short for serge-finishing; medium for gathering

**Stitch width:** Narrow to medium for serge-finishing; wide for gathering

**Needle:** Size 11/75

### How-tos:

1 Adjust the serger to a short, narrow- to medium-width stitch. From the right side of the strips, serge-finish each long edge. Then serge-finish the short ends of each strip.

2 Adjust for gathering. Fold the strips lengthwise, right sides together. Guide the filler cord carefully under the back and over the front of the presser foot, between the needle and knives, or thread it through a special guide or foot. (See Figs. 4-1 and 4-2)

3 Serge slowly over the filler cord for a few inches, carefully guiding it between the needle and knives (or the two needles of a 3/4-thread stitch) without stitching into it or cutting it. Insert the fold of each strip under the presser foot and filler cord and continue serging. (Fig. 4-15)

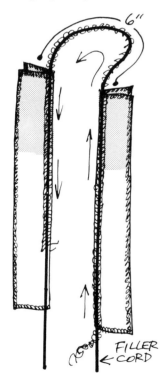

Fig. 4-15 *Continuously serge over the filler cord, catching the fold of each strip. Then clip the midpoint of the connecting threads.*

MOVE THE FABRIC SLIGHTLY AWAY FROM THE KNIVES WHEN SERGING TO AVOID CUTTING INTO IT. BE CAREFUL TO STITCH INTO THE FOLD BUT NOT INTO THE FILLER CORD.

4 Pull up the cord to gather the strip to a 6″ (15cm) length. Secure the cord ends by straight-stitching across them using a short stitch. Clip the excess thread chain and cord.

5 On each napkin ring, fold one end ³⁄₄″ (2cm) to the wrong side and lap it ³⁄₄″ (2cm) over the other end. Hand-stitch the ends together.

EMBELLISH THE RINGS, IF DESIRED, BY GLUING OR HAND-STITCHING A RIBBON AROUND THE CENTER, TYING THE ENDS INTO A BOW.

# RUFFLED BOW PILLOW

Put your serge-gathering skills to work to accent a sofa, chair, or bedroom with this unique pillow. (Fig. 4-16)

SKILLS USED:

Serged seams; serging outside corners; filler-cord gathering.

## Materials needed:

◆ 1¼ yard (1.1m) of tightly woven medium-weight fabric, such as chintz or calico

◆ Matching serger or all-purpose thread for the serging; matching all-purpose thread for the sewing machine

◆ Polyester fiberfill

◆ 3 yards (2.75m) of filler cord, such as pearl cotton or cotton crochet thread

◆ Seam sealant

## Cutting directions:

■ Cut two 18″ (46cm) squares for the pillow.

■ Cut one 45″ by 20″ (114cm by 51cm) rectangle for the ruffle.

■ Cut one 45″ by 2″ (114cm by 5cm) rectangle for the tie.

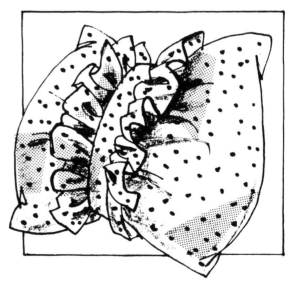

Fig. 4-16 *Highlight a plain pillow with a serge-gathered ruffle.*

3- or 3/4-thread balanced stitch

**Stitch length:** Medium

**Stitch width:** Wide

**Needle:** Size 11/75

### How-tos:

Serge-seam using ¼" (6mm) allowances, just skimming the edges with the knives.

1 Serge-seam the two squares wrong sides together, leaving a 5" (12.5cm) opening on one side for turning and stuffing. (See page 11 for techniques to begin and end the opening neatly.) At the corners, serge off the edge, pivot the fabric, and serge onto the adjoining edge. Dab seam sealant on the thread chains and clip the excess when dry.

**WHEN SERGING CORNERS, ANGLE THEM IN ABOUT 1/8" (3MM) ON BOTH SIDES OF THE POINT SO THEY'LL LOOK PERFECTLY SQUARE (SEE FIG. 3-16)**

2 Turn the pillow right side out and stuff it with fiberfill. Hand-stitch the opening closed.

3 Fold the ruffle lengthwise, right sides together, with the long raw edges meeting in the center. Serge-seam both short ends and turn the fabric right side out.

4 Guide the filler cord carefully under the back and over the front of the presser foot, between the needle and knives (or between the two needles of a 3/4-thread stitch), or thread it through a special guide or foot. (See Figs. 4-1 and 4-2)

5 Slowly serge over the filler cord for a few inches, carefully guiding it between needle and knives without stitching into it or cutting it. Fold the ruffle in half lengthwise with the raw edges positioned along one side and a fold of fabric between them. Insert the side of the ruffle with the raw edges under the presser foot and filler cord and continue serging, just skimming the edge and catching all layers in the stitching. (Fig. 4-17)

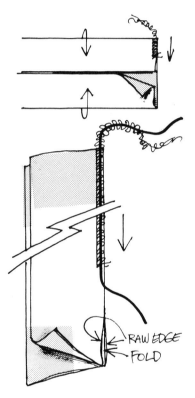

*Fig. 4-17 Serge over the filler cord as you seam the raw edges together.*

6 At the end, raise the needle and presser foot, pull the filler cord behind the needle, and chain off.

7 Secure one end of the cord by wrapping it around a pin or by straight-stitching back and forth across it. Pull the other end to gather the ruffle to 18" (46cm).

8 Center the wrong side of the ruffle on the right side of the pillow top.

9 Fold the tie rectangle lengthwise, with wrong sides together, and serge-seam the long edges.

10 Refold the tie with the seam centered lengthwise on the strip.

11 Beginning at the center back of the pillow, wrap the tie tightly around the pillow top, over the ruffle. (You may need to trim the tie to fit, depending on how full you've stuffed the pillow.) Turn the final tie end ¾" (2cm) to the wrong side and lap it over the beginning end. Hand-stitch the ends together securely. (Fig. 4-18)

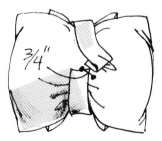

*Fig. 4-18 Hand-stitch the lapped ends of the tie together, gathering in the center of the pillow.*

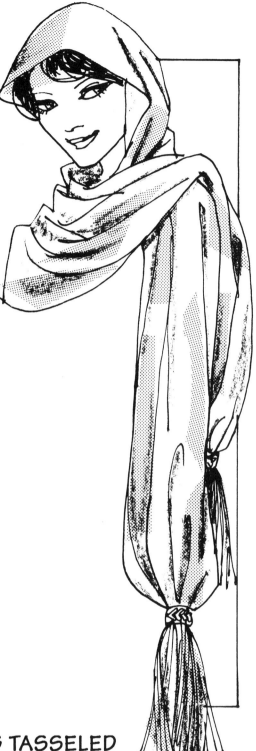

## LONG TASSELED SCARF

Whip up this sensational scarf. It's super-long and super-simple, too. (Fig. 4-19)

### SKILLS USED:

Serged seams; serged, turned, and top-stitched hems; filler-cord gathering.

*Fig. 4-19 Use a lightweight, loosely woven fabric that will fringe easily.*

## Materials needed:

◆ 1¹⁄₃ yard (1.25m) of 45"-wide (114cm) or wider loosely woven light- or medium-weight wool or acrylic fabric

◆ 10" (25.5cm) of ³⁄₄"-wide (2cm) decorative contrasting-color braid

◆ 1¹⁄₂ yard (1.5m) of matching pearl cotton or cotton crochet thread for filler cord

◆ Matching serger or all-purpose thread for serging; matching all-purpose thread for the sewing machine

◆ Seam sealant

◆ Air-erasable marker

## Cutting directions:

■ Cut two 40" by 24" (101.5cm by 61cm) rectangles from the fabric.

■ Cut the braid into two 5" (12.5cm) sections.

### SERGER SETTINGS:

3-thread balanced stitch

**Stitch length:** Medium

**Stitch width:** Medium

**Needle:** Size 11/75

## How-tos:

Serge-seam using ¹⁄₄" (6mm) allowances, trimming if necessary.

1 With right sides together, serge-seam two short ends together to form a long scarf. Steam-press the seam allowance toward one side.

2 On both long sides, lightly mark a point 10" (25.5cm) from each end. Serge-finish both long edges between the markings. (Fig. 4-20)

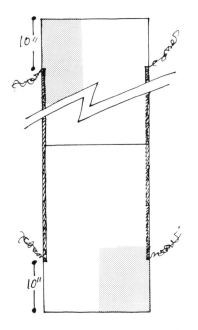

Fig. 4-20 Leave 10" unstitched on both ends where the scarf will be fringed.

*TO BEGIN THE SERGING, RAISE THE PRESSER FOOT AND NEEDLE AND PULL THE THREAD CHAIN FROM THE STITCH FINGER. POSITION THE FABRIC EDGE UNDER THE PRESSER FOOT, LOWERING THE NEEDLE INTO THE FABRIC AT ONE MARKING. WHEN YOU REACH THE OTHER MARKING, NEATLY CHAIN OFF BY RAISING THE PRESSER FOOT AND THE NEEDLE, PULLING THE FABRIC BEHIND THE NEEDLE AND CHAINING OFF. (SEE FIG. I-24)*

3 Press ¼" (6mm) of the serge-finished edges to the wrong side on the serging needleline. Then fold the edge the same amount again, enclosing the serge-finishing. Top-stitch approximately ⅛" (3mm) from the fold to hem the scarf sides to within 10" (25.5cm) of both ends.

4 Fold and press back both ends 10" (25.5cm), toward the right side of the scarf.

5 Slowly serge over two strands of filler cords for a few inches, carefully guiding it between the needle and knives without stitching into it or cutting it. (See Fig. 4-1)

*USE A SPECIAL GUIDE OR FOOT TO POSITION THE FILLER CORD ACCURATELY, IF ONE IS AVAILABLE FOR YOUR SERGER MODEL. (SEE FIG. 4-2)*

6 Insert one folded fabric edge under the presser foot and filler cord and continue serging. At the end of the fabric, raise the needle and presser foot, pull the filler cord behind the needle, and chain off. Repeat for the other end of the scarf. (Fig. 4-21)

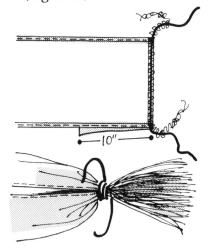

Fig. 4-21 Before fringing both ends, serge over the filler cord at the end of the side hems.

7 Fringe the scarf ends by gently pulling out the horizontal threads to the line of serging.

8 Secure both filler cords on one side by wrapping them around a pin or by straight-stitching back and forth across them. Pull the cords from the other edge to gather the fabric as tightly as possible.

9 Knot the cord ends to secure the gathering. Dab seam sealant on the knot and clip the excess thread when dry. Pull the fringed ends out and away from the scarf.

10 Beginning on the back of the scarf, wrap one braid section tightly around each gathering point, folding the braid end ½" (1.3cm) to the wrong side and lapping it over the beginning end. Hand-stitch the braid ends together and to the scarf underneath. Also hand-stitch the braid to the scarf at least once more, directly opposite the ends.

## PADDED FLOWER-POT COVER

Dress up a plain-looking or chipped flower pot with a simple padded cover. (Fig. 4-22)

**SKILLS USED:**

Serged, turned, and top-stitched hem; serging in a circle; serge-shirring.

## Materials needed:

◆ One circle of medium-weight woven fabric, such as calico or chintz, with a diameter equal to the pot's outer sides and bottom measurement plus 4" (10cm) (Fig. 4-23)

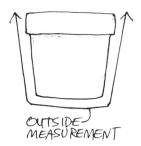

OUTSIDE MEASUREMENT

*Fig. 4-23 Add 4" to the pot's outside measurement when cutting the fabric circle. Cut the fleece without adding 4".*

*Fig. 4-22 Serge-shirr over narrow elastic so that the cover can be slipped on and off easily*

◆ One circle of polyester fleece, with a diameter equal to the pot's outer measurement only

◆ ⅛"-wide (3mm) elastic, the circumference of the pot plus 12" (30.5cm)

◆ Matching serger or all-purpose thread for serging; matching all-purpose thread for the sewing machine

◆ 1"-wide (2.5cm) ribbon in a contrasting color, equal to the circumference of the pot plus 18" (46cm)

◆ Air-erasable marker

**SERGER SETTINGS:**

3- or 3/4 thread balanced stitch

**Stitch length:** Medium

**Stitch width:** Wide

**Needle:** Size 11/75

## How-tos:

1 Adjust the differential feed to 1.5 or lengthen the stitch and tighten the needle-thread tension slightly. Serge-finish the edge of the fabric circle, lapping the stitches for 1" (2.5cm) at the end. Raise the presser foot and needle, pull the fabric behind the presser foot, and chain off. (See Fig. 1-24)

2 Press the width of the serge-finishing to the wrong side and top-stitch ⅛" (3mm) from the folded edge.

3 Mark an inner circle 1¼" (3cm) from the hemmed edge on the wrong side of the fabric. Fold the edge toward the center of the circle, right sides together, on the marked line.

4 Thread the elastic under the back and over the front of the presser foot between the needle and the knives (as you would for filler cord) or thread it through a special guide or foot. (See Figs. 4-1 and 4-2) Serge carefully over several inches of the elastic, being careful not to stitch into it or cut it.

5 Place the fabric fold under the presser foot and elastic. As you serge over it, be careful to stitch into the fold but not into the elastic.

*MOVE THE FABRIC FOLD SLIGHTLY AWAY FROM THE KNIVES WHEN SERGING TO AVOID CUTTING INTO IT.*

**6** Serge around to the starting position, pulling the beginning end of the elastic to the left of the needle to avoid serging through it or cutting it. To avoid stitching through or over the final elastic end, raise the presser foot and needle and pull the remaining elastic under the back of the foot behind the needle. Then gently pull the fabric behind the needle and chain off. (Fig. 4-24)

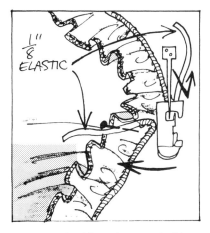

**Fig. 4-24** *Avoid cutting or stitching into the elastic so that it can be gathered later.*

**7** Center the fleece circle on the wrong side of the fabric circle. Center the pot on top of the fleece and pull up the elastic ends to fit snuggly. Knot the ends securely and clip them to 2" (5cm). Tuck the ends inside the cover.

**8** Wrap the ribbon tightly around the shirring and tie a bow at the front of the pot. Glue, pin, or hand-stitch the ribbon to the pot cover to secure it.

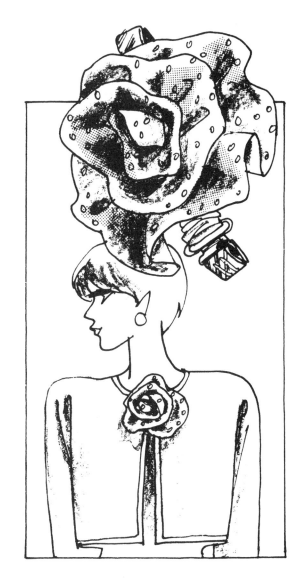

# FASHIONABLE ROSETTE CINCHER

Add a large fabric rosette to an elastic cincher with clips on both ends. It attaches anywhere on a garment as a decorative accent or fashionably holds together the front of a button-less jacket or coat. (Fig. 4-25)

### SKILLS USED:

For the rosette—differential-feed gathering; needle-thread gathering. For the optional cincher—serged seams; serge-finished edges.

**Fig. 4-25** *Put your serge-gathering skills to work to make this popular fashion accessory.*

### Materials needed:

◆ ⅙ yard (.2m) of 60"-wide (152cm) soft, lightweight fabric, such as chiffon, lace, or gauze

◆ Matching serger or all-purpose thread for serging

◆ One purchased cincher or make a cincher using a 7" by 2½" (18cm by 6.5cm) rectangle of medium-weight fabric (such as taffeta or faille), 3½" (9cm) of ¾"-wide (2cm) elastic, one set of suspender clips, and seam sealant

**SERGER SETTINGS:**

3-thread balanced stitch

**Stitch length:** Long

**Stitch width:** Medium to wide

**Needle:** Size 11/75

## How-tos:

*1* Adjust the differential feed to the highest setting and tighten the needle tension slightly.

*2* Fold the rosette fabric in half lengthwise, wrong sides together. Tapering the corners, serge-gather the cut edges, allowing the fabric to feed freely into the serger. (Fig. 4-26)

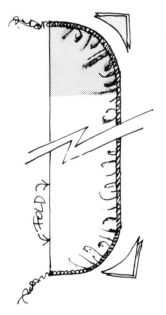

*Fig. 4-26 Gather and serge-finish the edges simultaneously using the differential feed.*

*3* Run your fingers along the chain at both ends to smooth out the loops. Find the shortest thread in both chains (the needle thread) and pull it from both ends to gather the rosette tightly. Knot the threads at both ends and clip the excess. (Fig. 4-27)

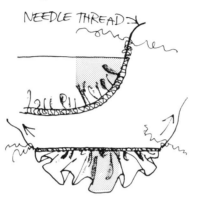

*Fig. 4-27 Pull the needle thread for additional gathering.*

*4* Beginning at one end, roll the serged edges, shaping the strip into a rosette. Hand-stitch the serged edges together and hand-stitch the rosette to a purchased cincher.

To make the cincher instead of using a purchased one:

*1* Adjust the differential feed and the needle tension to normal and the stitch length to medium. Fold the fabric in half lengthwise, right sides together, and serge-seam the long edges using a ¼" (6mm) seam allowance.

*2* Turn the fabric right side out and refold the tube so that the seam is centered on one long side. Press lightly and insert the elastic into the tube.

*3* Matching the cut edges of the elastic and the tube, serge-finish one end, making sure to catch the elastic in the serging.

*4* Slide the tube over the elastic to match all the cut edges on the opposite end of the tube. Serge-finish, catching the elastic in the serging. Dab seam sealant at the ends of the serging. Clip the excess thread chain when dry. (Fig. 4-28)

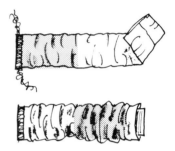

*Fig. 4-28 Line up the remaining cut edges of the tube and elastic before serge-finishing them together.*

*5* Push the fabric toward the center of the elastic tube and thread the ends through the clips, folding ½" (1.3cm) to the wrong side. Straight-stitch through the serging to secure them. (Fig. 4-29)

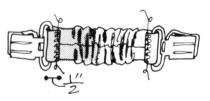

*Fig. 4-29 Smooth out the tube ends before threading them through the clips.*

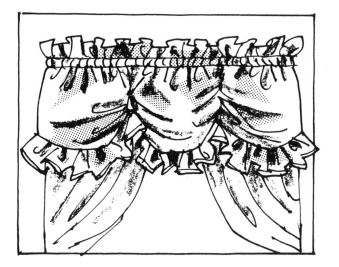

# CHARMING SWAG VALANCE

Easily serge a ruffled and gathered valance to fit any size window. (Fig. 4-30)

### SKILLS USED:

Serged seams; serged, turned, and top-stitched hems; filler-cord gathering; differential-feed gathering.

## Materials needed:

◆ Lightweight woven fabric approximately 1½ to 2 times the window width by ⅞ yard (.8m), for the valance and ruffle.

*FOR A LIGHTWEIGHT FABRIC, YOU'LL WANT ABOUT TWICE THE WINDOW WIDTH, BUT LESS WORKS WELL FOR HEAVIER FABRIC. APPROXIMATE MEASUREMENTS ARE OKAY, SO IF YOUR FABRIC IS A LITTLE WIDER OR NARROWER, DON'T WORRY. FOR A WIDE WINDOW, YOU MAY NEED TO PIECE THE FABRIC TO GIVE THE VALANCE ENOUGH FULLNESS.*

◆ Matching serger or all-purpose thread for serging; matching all-purpose thread for the sewing machine

*Fig. 4-30 Serging makes valances and other home decorating a breeze.*

◆ 3 yards (2.75m) of filler cord, such as pearl cotton or cotton crochet thread

◆ Seam sealant

## Cutting directions:

■ For the valance, cut one rectangle the desired width (1½ to 2 times the window width) by 22" (56cm). Piece if necessary.

■ For the ruffle, cut one rectangle two times the width of the valance rectangle by 4" (10cm). Piece if necessary.

*TO PIECE THE VALANCE AND/OR RUFFLE RECTANGLES, PLACE TWO SHORT ENDS RIGHT SIDES TOGETHER AND SERGE-SEAM.*

### SERGER SETTINGS:

3- or 3/4-thread balanced stitch

**Stitch length:** Medium

**Stitch width:** Wide

**Needle:** Size 11/75

## How-tos:

Serge-seam using ¼" (6mm) allowances, just skimming the edges with the knives.

1 Serge-finish the upper edge of the valance rectangle, the lower edge of the ruffle rectangle, and the short ends of both rectangles.

2 Hem the lower ruffle edge by pressing ⅜" (1cm) to the wrong side and top-stitching ¼" (6mm) from the folded edge. Repeat for the short ends of the ruffle and the valance.

3 At the upper edge of the valance, press 3¼" (8cm) to the wrong side. Top-stitch through the serged edge, forming a hem.

4 Top-stitch through the hem 1½" (4cm) from the upper edge to create the upper ruffle and the rod casing.

5 Press-mark the valance into vertical thirds. (Fig. 4-31)

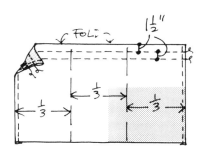

*Fig. 4-31 Mark the valance where the filler-cord gathering will be done.*

6 Guide the filler cord carefully under the back and over the front of the presser foot, between the needle and knives (or between the two needles of a 3/4-thread stitch). (See Fig. 4-1) Serge slowly over the filler cord for a few inches without stitching into it or cutting it. Fold the valance, right sides together, on the third markings and insert the fabric fold, raw edge first, under the presser foot and filler cord. Continue serging to ½" (1.3cm) from the serge-finished hem casing. Raise the needle and presser foot, pull the fabric behind the needle, and chain off. Secure the filler and chain at the lower edge by dabbing seam sealant on the edge of the fabric. Do NOT cut the chain or the filler cord.

*MOVE THE FABRIC FOLD SLIGHTLY AWAY FROM THE KNIVES WHEN SERGING TO AVOID CUTTING INTO IT.*

7 Adjust to a long stitch and the highest differential-feed setting. Serge along the ruffle's upper edge, allowing the fabric to feed freely into the machine for serge-gathering.

*INCREASE THE AMOUNT OF GATHERING BY TIGHTENING THE NEEDLE TENSION SLIGHTLY OR EASE-PLUS. (SEE FIG. 1-17)*

8 Place the ruffle and valance right sides together with the ruffle on top and adjust the gathers evenly to fit. If the ruffle still needs additional gathering, gently pull on the needle thread (the shortest thread in the thread chain) until both edges are the same length.

9 Adjust the serger back to normal needle tension and differential-feed settings and shorten the stitch length to medium. Serge-seam the ruffle to the valance, catching the thread chains and filler cord in the seaming. Knot the thread chains at both ends and dab seam sealant on the knots. Clip the excess thread when dry.

10 To secure the filler cords in the serge-seaming, straight-stitch over them using a short stitch length.

11 Pull the upper end of the filler cords, gathering the two vertical rows to an attractive length. Thread the filler cord into a large-eyed needle and hand-stitch it securely to the bottom of the valance's upper hem, knotting it to the loose thread chain. Trim the excess threads. (Fig. 4-32)

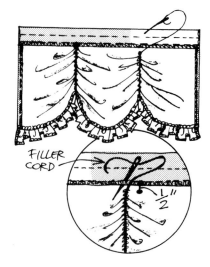

Fig. 4-32 *Secure the gathering by hand-stitching the filler cord to the casing hem.*

# Notes

# 5 Serged Knit Know-how

Your serger is ideal for sewing knits because it can finish seams and edges neatly without stretching them, and the serged stitch will stretch with the give of the knit fabric. Because 3- and 3/4-thread serged stitches stretch the most, they are preferable for serging knits. (Fig. 5-1)

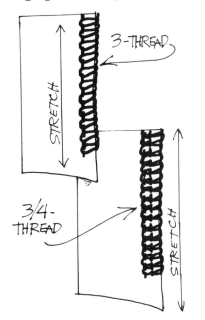

*Fig. 5-1 Serge knits using one of these stretchable stitches.*

*IF YOUR MACHINE HAS A DIFFERENTIAL FEED, IT WILL BE VERY HELPFUL FOR SERGING KNITS (SEE PAGE 8). FOR MORE IN-DEPTH INFORMATION, REFER TO CHAPTER 8 IN ABCS OF SERGING.*

When selecting fabric for a knit garment, compare the fabric's stretch to the requirements on the pattern envelope—most give a stretch ratio or gauge if the pattern is designed for knits. Because of the serger's stretchable stitch, you may use any thread with a fiber content appropriate for your fabric.

Because all knits don't stretch the same amount, it is important to test your stitching before serging the project. Test-seam on scraps of the project fabric, then stretch the fabric as it will be stretched during wear or use. If a thread breaks, it will probably be the needle thread. Loosen the needle-thread tension(s) a little or stretch slightly while serging to allow the stitching more give. Another option is to use a strong stretchable thread such as woolly nylon in the needle(s).

*USE A FINE-GAUGE NEEDLE THREADER (OR THE MACHINE'S BUILT-IN THREADER) TO HELP FEED THIS SOFT, CRIMPED THREAD THROUGH THE NEEDLE EYE.*

Preshrink any washable knit fabric with the exception of "needle-ready" sweatering and nylon/Lycra. Don't preshrink elastic or ribbing.

Always begin your project with a sharp new needle. This is especially important on knits to prevent holes or snagging along the seamline. If you have trouble with skipped stitches, check to see if your dealer recommends a ball-point needle for your serger model. When top-stitching knits with a conventional sewing machine, try a new "stretch" single or twin-needle to avoid skipped stitches.

If a knit edge stretches as you serge over it, use the differential feed on a higher setting or ease-plus the fabric to prevent it.

When serging ribbing, use a long stitch and serge with the ribbing on top to let the feed dogs help ease the garment or project fabric to the ribbing. Use the same technique for applying sew-through or clear elastic.

*FOR DETAILED INFORMATION ON RIBBING APPLICATION, SEE CHAPTER 4 IN SERGED GARMENTS IN MINUTES, INCLUDING THE "RIBBING GUIDELINES" CHART ON PAGE 42.*

## JIFFY
## RIBBED-NECK
## NIGHTSHIRT

Use a nightshirt pattern or
lengthen a basic T-shirt pattern
to make this easy and comfortable sleeper. (Fig. 5-2)

### SKILLS USED:

Serged seams; circular ribbing
application; serged, turned, and
top-stitched hems; twin-needle
top-stitching.

*Fig. 5-2 Make a T-shirt following
the same simple instructions.*

## Materials needed:

◆ Nightshirt or basic oversized
T-shirt pattern with a ribbed
crew neckline, dropped
shoulders, and hems on the
sleeves and lower edge

SELECT THE PATTERN SIZE BY
COMPARING YOUR BUST
MEASUREMENT TO THOSE ON
THE BACK OF THE PATTERN
ENVELOPE. THE ACTUAL BUST
MEASUREMENT WILL INCLUDE
BOTH WEARING AND DESIGN
EASE, AND MAY BE PRINTED ON
THE FRONT PATTERN PIECE.

◆ Knit yardage, following the
pattern specifications and
yardage requirements—
purchase extra if you will be
lengthening a T-shirt pattern

◆ Matching or contrasting
ribbing, following the
pattern yardage
requirements

◆ Matching serger or all-
purpose thread for serging;
matching all-purpose thread
for the sewing machine

◆ Twin-needle for the sewing
machine

## Cutting directions:

■ Adjust the finished length
of the garment, if desired,
especially if you're using a
T-shirt pattern. Compare
your measurements to the
back-length measurement
listed on the pattern envelope. If necessary, lengthen
or shorten at the bottom
edge of both the front and
back pattern pieces.

■ Cut one back, one front, and
two sleeves from the fabric.

■ Cut the ribbing with the
greatest stretch running the
length of the ribbed band,
following the pattern piece
or measurements from the
pattern instructions.

■ If the pattern calls for ⅝"
(1.5cm) seam allowances on
the ribbing and neckline
edges, trim both to ¼"
(6mm).

3- or 3/4-thread balanced stitch

**Stitch length:** Medium

**Stitch width:** Wide

**Needle:** Size 11/75

## How-tos:

When serge-seaming ¼″ (6mm) allowances, just skim the fabric edge with the knives. When the allowances are ⅝″ (1.5cm), serge-seam with the needle (the left needle of a 3/4-thread machine) on the seam-line and trim approximately ⅜″ (1cm) with the knives.

1 With right sides together, serge both shoulder seams continuously, without raising the presser foot. Leave about 4″ of thread chain between the seams and clip the middle of the thread chains afterward to separate the sections. Press the seam allowances toward the back.

2 Using a ¼″ (6mm) seam allowance, straight-stitch the ribbing short ends to form a circle. Finger-press the seam allowances open.

3 Fold the ribbing circle in half lengthwise, wrong sides together.

4 Using pins, quartermark the ribbing and the neckline edge by folding them in quarters, placing one quartermark at the center back.

*THE SHOULDER SEAMS ARE USUALLY NOT HALFWAY BETWEEN THE CENTER FRONT AND CENTER BACK, SO THEY WILL NOT BE ON THE QUARTERMARKS.*

5 Align the ribbing and garment cut edges, placing the ribbing seam at the center back. Match and pin the ribbing and garment at the other quartermarks. Adjust to a long stitch. Raise the presser foot and needle and insert the neckline edge under the foot at one side quartermark with the ribbing on top and the needle in the seamline. Serge-seam the ribbing to the opening, removing the pins just before they reach the foot and stretching the ribbing to fit between the quartermarks. Overlap the beginning serging for 1/2″ (1.3cm) and chain off. Clip the excess thread chain. (Fig. 5-3)

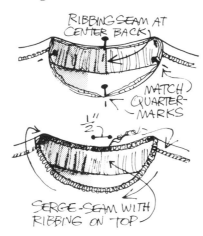

*Fig. 5-3 Lap the serging for ¹/₂″ to finish the seam.*

*ADJUST THE DIFFERENTIAL FEED TO ITS HIGHEST SETTING TO HELP EASE THE GARMENT TO THE RIBBING AND TO AVOID STRETCHING THE RIBBING EXCESSIVELY.*

6 Carefully steam and finger-press the seam allowance toward the garment, without touching the ribbing with the iron.

*TO ADD DURABILITY, TOP-STITCH THROUGH THE SEAM ALLOWANCE FROM THE RIGHT SIDE, USING A LONG STITCH AND STRETCHING AS YOU SEW. OR USE TWIN-NEEDLE TOP-STITCHING FOR AN "AUTOMATIC" STRETCH.*

7 Adjust the serger to a medium-length stitch and the differential feed to 1.5. Serge-finish the lower edge of both sleeves from the right side of the fabric.

8 With right sides together and the markings matching, serge-seam the sleeves to the garment with the garment on top. Press the seam allowances toward the sleeves and the sleeve hem allowances to the wrong side. Open the hem allowances flat.

9 Beginning at the lower edge with right sides together and matching the underarm seams, serge one sleeve/side seam. Press the seam allowance toward the back.

*WHEN SERGE-SEAMING STRIPED FABRIC, ALLOW A SCANT 1/8″ (3MM) OF THE FABRIC UNDER-LAYER TO SHOW SO THAT YOU CAN ACCURATELY MATCH THE STRIPES AS YOU SERGE. (FIG. 5-4)*

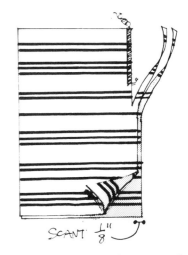

*Fig. 5-4 Let the underlayer extend slightly to match stripes without basting.*

10  Serge-finish the lower hem edge.

11  Serge the other sleeve/side seam. Press the seam allowances toward the back.

12  Press the lower hem allowance to the wrong side and turn the sleeve hems up on the pressed lines.

13  Using the twin-needle and a long stitch, top-stitch the lower and sleeve hems from the right side. (Fig. 5-5)

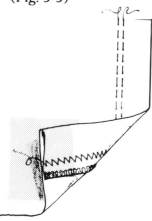

*Fig. 5-5  The twin-needle top-stitching stretches with the fabric because of the zigzag of the bobbin thread on the underside.*

# QUICK PULL-ON LEGGINGS

Serge these simple leggings for a fashionable look or use the same techniques for any basic pull-on pants. (Fig. 5-6)

SKILLS USED:

Serged seams; serged, turned, and top-stitched hems; inserted elastic application; twin-needle top-stitching.

*Fig. 5-6  Quickly serge leggings or any basic pull-on pant style.*

## Materials needed:

♦ Legging (or pants) pattern featuring an elasticized waistline and machine-stitched hems

♦ Stretch knit fabric with some *Lycra* content, following the pattern specifications and yardage requirements

♦ Sew-through waistline elastic, the length specified on the pattern in a width you prefer.

A WIDER ELASTIC WILL PROVIDE MORE CONTROL AT THE WAIST-LINE THAN A NARROWER ELASTIC. SELECT THE WIDTH OF ELASTIC YOU PREFER AND MAKE THE NECESSARY ADJUSTMENTS TO THE PATTERN BEFORE CUTTING.

♦ Matching serger or all-purpose thread for serging; matching all-purpose thread for the sewing machine

♦ Twin-needle for the sewing machine

## Cutting directions:

■ If the elastic width is different than specified in the pattern requirements, adjust both the front and back pattern pieces for a waistline casing double the elastic width plus ½" (1.3cm).

■ If you are unsure of your crotch depth, add to the waistline casing width (you can always trim after fitting). Cut the casing straight up from the top of the waistline edges.

■ Cut out two fronts and two backs (or two front/back pieces if the pattern doesn't have side seams).

SERGER SETTINGS:

3- or 3/4-thread balanced stitch

**Stitch length:** Medium

**Stitch width:** Wide

**Needle:** Size 11/75

## How-tos:

When serge-seaming ¼" (6mm) allowances, just skim the fabric edge with the knives. When the allowances are ⅝" (1.5cm), serge-seam with the needle (the left needle of a 3/4-thread machine) on the seam-line and trim approximately ⅜" (1cm) with the knives.

1 If the pattern has side seams, place the front and back pieces right sides together. Serge-seam from the lower edge to the waistline. Press the seam allowances toward the back.

HOLD THE THREAD CHAIN TAUT AT THE LOWER EDGE WHEN BEGINNING TO SERGE TO PRE-VENT THE SEAM FROM PULLING UP. TO HOLD THE LONG EDGES IN PLACE FOR SERGING, PIN PARALLEL TO THE SEAMLINE ABOUT 1/2" (1.3CM) TO THE LEFT OF IT. BE CAREFUL TO REMOVE THE PINS BEFORE THEY REACH THE PRESSER FOOT. OR USE FINGER-PINNING, SECURING ONE END OF THE SEAMLINE WITH THE NEEDLE AND PRESSER FOOT AND HOLDING THE MATCHED EDGES AT THE SEAMLINE MIDPOINT AND THE LOWER EDGE. RELEASE THE FABRIC WHEN THE FOOT REACHES YOUR FINGERS. (FIG. 5-7)

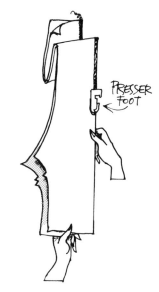

*Fig. 5-7 Serge seams without pinning by holding the edges together with your fingers.*

2 Serge-finish the lower hem edges and press the hem allowances to the wrong side.

3 Beginning at the lower edges of the hem allowances (after opening them flat), continuously serge the inseams on both legs, with right sides together. Hold the thread chain taut as you begin and clip the middle of the connecting chain when finished. (Fig. 5-8)

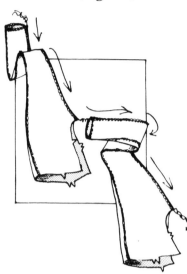

Fig. 5-8 *Continuously serge both inseams from the lower edge up.*

4 Turn one leg right side out and insert it inside the second leg. Serge-seam the crotch, matching the inseams.

**TO PREVENT THE CROTCH SEAM FROM BREAKING, STRETCH AS YOU SERGE THE CURVED AREA.**

5 Cut the elastic to fit comfortably around your waistline with ½" (1.3cm) extra. Lap the cut ends ½" (1.3cm) and zigzag them together.

6 Try on the leggings and place the elastic around your waistline on the outside. Pin the upper edge to the right side over the elastic. Test the crotch depth by sitting down and, if necessary, adjust the casing for a comfortable fit. Mark the casing foldline above the elastic, then mark the remainder of the casing equal to the elastic width plus ½" (1.3cm) and trim the excess fabric. Serge-finish the casing's raw edge. (Fig. 5-9)

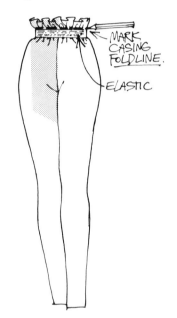

Fig. 5-9 *Mark the casing foldline at the top of the elastic*

7 Press the casing to the wrong side along the fold-line. Insert the circle of elastic under the fold and top-stitch the loose casing edge next to the elastic. (Fig. 5-10)

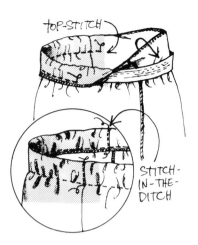

Fig. 5-10 *Top-stitch the casing edge next to, but not through, the elastic.*

8 Pull the elastic and fabric out to its maximum width and then release it to distribute the gathers evenly. From the right side, stitch-in-the-ditch at the front, back, and side seamlines to secure the elastic and prevent it from rolling in the casing.

**STRAIGHT-STITCH THROUGH THE ELASTIC VERTICALLY AT THE SIDES, EVEN IF YOUR PATTERN HAS NO SIDE SEAMS.**

9 Fold up the hems and top-stitch them in place from the right side, using a long stitch and a twin-needle to prevent the thread from breaking when the leggings are worn.

**IF YOU PREFER, YOU MAY USE A SINGLE NEEDLE AND A LONG STITCH, STRETCHING FIRMLY AS YOU SEW THE HEMS.**

# BASIC TANK SWIMSUIT

Once you've fitted the pattern to your measurements, making a swimsuit on your serger is a snap. (Fig. 5-11)

**SKILLS USED:**

Serged seams; swimsuit-elastic application.

## Materials needed:

◆ Basic tank swimsuit pattern with a scooped neckline in front and back

*Fig. 5-11 Your serger's stretchable stitch is ideal for making swimwear.*

**SELECT THE PATTERN SIZE BY COMPARING YOUR BUST MEASUREMENT TO THOSE ON THE BACK OF THE PATTERN ENVELOPE.**

◆ Nylon/*Lycra* knit fabric, following the pattern yardage requirements

◆ One 8″ by 9″ (20.5cm by 23cm) rectangle of swimsuit lining for the crotch

◆ ³/₈″-wide (1cm) swim elastic, following the pattern yardage requirements

◆ Matching serger or all-purpose thread for serging; matching all-purpose thread for the sewing machine

## Cutting directions:

■ Compare your body measurements to the pattern. Make any necessary alterations on both the front and back pattern pieces by dividing the difference between your measurements and the pattern measurements into the number of shorten/lengthen lines and adjusting accordingly.

■ Cut one front and a right and left back from the swimsuit fabric.

■ Cut one crotch lining from the swimsuit lining.

**SERGER SETTINGS:**

3- or 3/4-thread balanced stitch

**Stitch length:** Medium

**Stitch width:** Wide

**Needle:** Size 11/75

## How-tos:

When serge-seaming ¼″ (6mm) allowances, just skim the fabric edge with the knives. When the allowances are ⁵/₈″ (1.5cm), serge-seam with the needle (the left needle of a 3/4-thread machine) on the seamline and trim approximately ³/₈″ (1cm) with the knives.

1 With right sides together and the cut edges matching, serge-seam the two center backs together.

2 Straight-stitch the front and back, right sides together, at the crotch seamline, stretching as you stitch.

3 Place the right side back of the crotch lining over the wrong side of the back and serge-seam over the previous crotch-seam stitching. (Fig. 5-12)

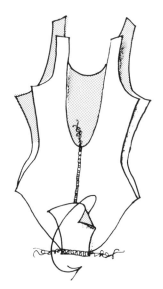

Fig. 5-12 *After serge-seaming the crotch lining, fold it back toward the front of the suit, covering the stitching.*

4 Fold the crotch lining over the seam allowance toward the suit front. Matching the cut edges, machine-baste the crotch lining along the front leg openings.

5 With right sides together, serge-seam the sides and the shoulders.

6 Measure and cut the elastic for the neckline, following the pattern instructions. Lap the elastic ends ½" (1.3cm) and zigzag them together. (Fig. 5-13)

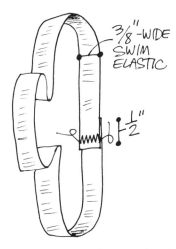

Fig. 5-13 *Zigzag the lapped ends together.*

7 Quartermark both the elastic and the neckline edge, placing one mark at the center back.

8 Adjust your serger to a long stitch. Raise the presser foot and needle and insert the elastic and fabric under the foot, with markings matching and the elastic over the wrong side of the fabric. Serge-seam, stretching the elastic to fit the neckline opening. Finish by serging over the beginning stitching for about ½" (1.3cm) before chaining off. (Fig. 5-14)

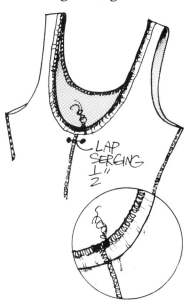

Fig. 5-14 *Apply elastic to the wrong side of a circular edge.*

**TO PREVENT THE KNIVES FROM NICKING THE ELASTIC, MOVE THE ELASTIC SLIGHTLY AWAY FROM THEM WHEN SERGING.**

9 Measure and cut the elastic for the armhole and leg openings. Lap and zigzag the pieces into circles. Apply the elastic to the suit, following the instructions in step 8.

10 On the neckline opening, fold the elastic to the wrong side with the loose edge of the elastic against the fold of the fabric. From the right side, top-stitch using a long stitch ¼" (6mm) from the folded edge, stretching as you sew and being sure to catch the elastic underneath. (Fig. 5-15)

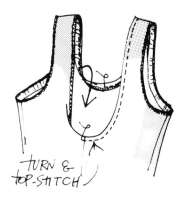

Fig. 5-15 *Stretch as you top-stitch to prevent the thread from breaking when the edge stretches during wear.*

**IF YOU PREFER, TOP-STITCH USING A TWIN-NEEDLE AND A LONG STITCH. STRETCH AS YOU SEW TO ADD MORE GIVE TO THE STITCHING.**

11 Repeat step 10 for the armhole and leg openings.

12 From the wrong side, steam well to shrink the elastic back to its original length, being careful not to touch the fabric with the iron.

## SENSATIONAL SARONG COVER-UP

Wrap up your swimming fashion image with a simple sarong. It's so easy that you can quickly serge one to match every suit. (Fig. 5-16)

Fig. 5-16 *Wrap the sarong ties around your waist, lapping the edges of the skirt to fit.*

### SKILLS USED:

Serged seams; serge-finished edges; lettuced edges; *Lycra* waistband application.

### Materials needed:

- ◆ One yard (.95m) of 45"-wide (114cm) nylon/*Lycra* knit fabric
- ◆ Matching serger or all-purpose thread for serging

### Cutting directions:

- ■ Cut one 45" by 22" (114cm by 56cm) fabric rectangle, with the greatest stretch running in the shorter crosswise direction.
- ■ Cut two 45" by 6" (114cm by 15cm) fabric strips, with the greatest stretch running across the width of the strips.

### SERGER SETTINGS:

3- or 3/4-thread balanced stitch

**Stitch length:** Short for seaming and lettucing; long for waistband application

**Stitch width:** Narrow for seaming and lettucing; wide for waistband application

**Needle:** Size 11/75

### How-tos:

Serge-seam using ¹/₄" (6mm) allowances, trimming if necessary.

*1* Serge-seam two short ends of the strips, right sides together, to form one long sash.

2 Adjust the serger to a short, narrow 3-thread stitch. Fold the sash in half lengthwise, wrong sides together. Serge-seam the short ends and, beginning from the ends, serge-seam the cut edges together for 22" (56cm) on both sides. At the end of both 22" sections, raise the presser foot and the needle, pull the fabric behind the needle, and chain off. (Fig. 5-17)

*Fig. 5-17 Serge-seam both ends of the sash.*

3 Round the two corners on one long edge of the large rectangle, using a large lid as a guide.

4 On the long rounded edge and the two adjoining sides, lightly press ³⁄₈" (1cm) to the wrong side.

5 Adjust the differential feed to the lowest setting. Beginning on the right side of one square corner, anchor several stitches into the fabric over the pressed fold. Then hold the thread chain behind the presser foot and the fabric edge in front of the foot and stretch the fabric evenly as you serge over it, lettucing the folded edge until you reach the opposite square corner. (Fig. 5-18)

*Fig. 5-18 Lettuce the skirt's outer edges over a fold for durability.*

6 Adjust the serger to a long, wide stitch. Quartermark the unfinished edge of the large rectangle and the unfinished edges of the sash. With the sash on the top, serge-seam the sash to the sarong, stretching it to match the sarong quartermarks and using the differential feed on a setting slightly higher than normal to help ease the skirt to the band. (Fig. 5-19)

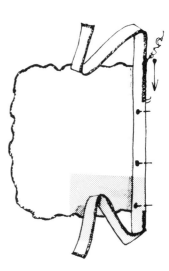

*Fig. 5-19 Stretch the sash to meet the quartermarks on the sarong.*

# ABSORBENT STRETCH-TERRY HEADBAND

Whip up a thirsty headband to use during your workout or to hold your hair out of the way when washing your face or applying makeup. (Fig. 5-20)

*Fig. 5-20 Make a practical headband with an unusual twist.*

Serged seams; thread-chain turning.

## Materials needed:

◆ One 30″ by 4½″ (76cm by 11.5cm) rectangle of stretch terry or velour fabric, with the greater stretch running lengthwise on the strip

*COTTON/LYCRA STRETCH TERRY OR VELOUR IS MORE ABSORBENT THAN BLENDS CONTAINING BOTH POLYESTER AND COTTON.*

◆ Matching serger or all-purpose thread for serging

## Cutting directions:

Determine the band length by knotting the strip and wrapping it around your head comfortably. Cut the strip to that measurement, adding ¼″ (6mm) seam allowances on all sides.

*THE LENGTH OF THE HEADBAND WILL VARY WITH THE BULK AND STRETCH OF THE FABRIC YOU'RE USING.*

SERGER SETTINGS:

3- or 3/4-thread balanced stitch

**Stitch length:** Medium

**Stitch width:** Wide

**Needle:** Size 11/75

## How-tos:

Serge-seam using ¼″ (6mm) allowances, just skimming the edges with the knives..

1 Serge a 30″ thread chain, but do not cut it. Fold the band in half lengthwise, right sides together, and place the chain between the layers. Raise the presser foot and needle and insert the band's cut edges approximately 1½″ (4cm) from the end. Serge-seam the length of the strip to approximately 1½″ (4cm) from the other end. Raise the presser foot and the needle, pull the fabric behind the needle, and chain off. (Fig. 5-21)

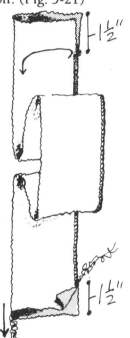

*Fig. 5-21 Leave a short section unserged at both ends.*

*PLACE THE THREAD CHAIN NEAR THE FOLD OF THE FABRIC INSIDE THE BAND TO AVOID CUTTING IT WHILE SERGE-SEAMING.*

2 Gently pull on the thread chain, easing the fabric through the band to turn it right side out.

3 Center the seam lengthwise on one side of the band and press lightly. Knot the middle of the band with the seamline on the back side, adjusting the knot so that it feels comfortable against your head.

4 Serge-seam the short ends of the band, right sides together. (Fig. 5-22)

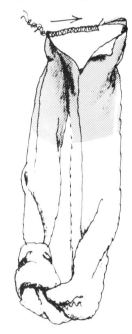

*Fig. 5-22 Fit the band and make any necessary adjustments before serge-seaming the ends together.*

5 Hand-stitch the opening closed.

*USING THE SAME TECHNIQUES, ELIMINATE THE KNOT AND VARY THE WIDTH TO MAKE PLAIN HEAD OR WRIST SWEATBANDS.*

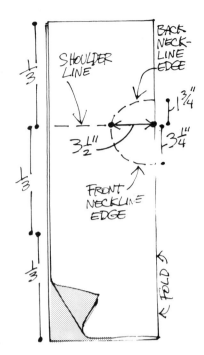

Fig. 5-24 *Position the shoulder line closer to the bib back, making the bib front longer.*

**BEFORE APPLYING THE RIBBING, FIT THE BIB OVER THE BABY'S HEAD TO MAKE SURE IT WILL PULL ON EASILY. IF IT DOESN'T, TRIM OUT THE FRONT NECKLINE EDGE SLIGHTLY.**

■ Test the ribbing length by marking and holding the ends together at 14" (35.5cm) and fitting it over the baby's head. Adjust the length for an easy fit, if necessary, and trim the excess.

**SERGER SETTINGS:**

3- or 3/4-thread balanced stitch

**Stitch length:** Medium to long

**Stitch width:** Wide

**Needle:** Size 11/75

# EFFORTLESS TERRY-TOWEL BIB

You can make this absorbent terry-cloth bib in a jiffy to slip easily over baby's head—no snaps or ties to fiddle with! (Fig. 5-23)

SKILLS USED:

Serged seams; circular ribbing application.

## Materials needed:

◆ One terry hand or kitchen towel

◆ 16" by 3" (40.5cm by 7.5cm) of ribbing, with the greatest stretch running lengthwise on the strip

Fig. 5-23 *Combine a terry towel and a strip of ribbing to make a practical bib.*

◆ Matching serger or all-purpose thread for serging; matching all-purpose thread for the sewing machine

◆ Air-erasable marker

## Cutting directions:

■ Fold the towel in half lengthwise and then in thirds crosswise. Establish the shoulder line by lightly marking one of the crosswise folds, using the marker. From that line, mark and trim out the neckline, following the illustration. (Fig. 5-24)

## How-tos:

Serge-seam using ¼" (6mm) allowances, just skimming the edges with the knives.

1 Serge-seam the short ends of the ribbing, right sides together, to form a circle.

2 Fold the ribbing circle in half lengthwise, wrong sides together.

3 Using pins, quartermark the ribbing and the neckline opening by folding them in quarters, placing one quartermark at the center back of both.

4 With right sides together and the ribbing on top, match the quartermarks and place the ribbing seam at the bib center back. Raise the presser foot and needle and insert the bib and ribbing under the foot. Serge-seam the neckline opening, removing the pins before they reach the foot. Finish by overlapping the beginning serging about ½" (1.3cm) before chaining off. (See Fig. 5-3)

*AS YOU LAP THE SERGING, BE CAREFUL NOT TO CUT THE BEGINNING STITCHES. WHEN SERGING OVER THEM, MOVE THE FABRIC SLIGHTLY TO THE LEFT OF THE KNIVES.*

5 Carefully press the seam allowance toward the bib without touching the iron to the ribbing. For durability, top-stitch next to the ribbing, stretching as you stitch and catching the seam allowance underneath.

# SNUGGLY SLIPPER SOX

Keep your feet warm and toasty with these washable, easy-to-serge treats. (Fig. 5-25)

### SKILLS USED:

Serged seams; elastic gathering; serging faux fur.

## Materials needed:

◆ One pair of washable knit socks

◆ 4" (10cm) of washable faux fur with a knit backing

◆ ⅔ yard (.6m) of ⅜"-wide (1cm) or wider clear elastic

◆ Matching serger or all-purpose thread for serging

## Cutting directions:

■ Stretch the top of one sock and measure the circumference.

■ Cut two faux fur rectangles 4" (10cm) by the length of the circumference measurement plus ½" (1.3cm) for seam allowances.

*TO KEEP THE FAUX FUR FROM SHEDDING AT THE EDGES, IMMEDIATELY SERGE-FINISH ALL THE EDGES OF THE RECTANGLES.*

### SERGER SETTINGS:

3- or 3/4-thread balanced stitch

**Stitch length:** Long

**Stitch width:** Wide

**Needle:** Size 11/75

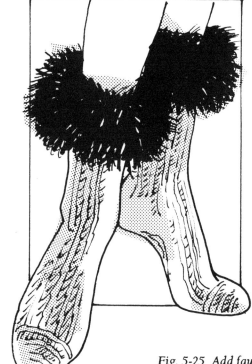

*Fig. 5-25 Add faux fur cuffs to ready-made socks.*

## How-tos:

Serge-seam using ¼″ (6mm) allowances, just skimming the edges with the knives.

1 Serge-seam the short ends of both faux fur rectangles, forming circles.

2 On both socks, quartermark the upper sock edge and one long edge of the faux fur circle, using any method that is clearly visible. Place the right side of the faux fur against the wrong side of the upper sock edge, matching the markings. Adjust the serger to the highest differential setting. Raise the presser foot and the needle and place the sock and faux fur under the foot, with the sock on the top. Serge-seam the edge, stretching the sock to fit the faux fur. (Fig. 5-26)

*Fig. 5-26  Stretch the sock to the faux fur as you serge-seam them together.*

WHEN SERGING, EASE THE FAUX FUR TO THE SOCK ON TOP OF IT TO AVOID STRETCHING OUT THE UPPER SOCK EDGE.

3 Stretch the elastic several times and measure it around your leg where the faux fur's lower edge will be. Mark this length, plus ½″ (1.3cm) for the overlap, on the clear elastic. Do not cut the elastic.

4 Quartermark the elastic and the unfinished faux fur edge on one sock. Match the markings, placing the elastic on the wrong-side unfinished edge of the faux fur. Leave the differential feed at its highest setting. Raise the presser foot and needle and place the edge under the foot. Serge a few stitches on the elastic and faux fur, then stretch the elastic to the first marking before serging through it.

5 At each marking, stretch the elastic to the next marking as you serge it to the edge. Lap the elastic and beginning stitching ½″ (1.3cm), then trim off the excess elastic. Repeat for the other sock. (Fig. 5-27)

LAP ELASTIC ENDS ½″

*Fig. 5-27  Serge the stretched elastic to the loose cuff edge to hold it snuggly in place.*

6 With the iron approximately 1″ (2.5cm) above the faux fur, steam well to shrink it.

7 Turn the elasticized edge to the wrong side and hand-stitch it to the faux fur underside at the quarter-marks. Then turn the cuff down.

# SOFT-TEXTURED BATH MITT

Give your skin a gentle massage as you bathe or shower with this fitted mitt. A ribbed cuff holds it in place. (Fig. 5-28)

**SKILLS USED:**

Serged seams; serging curves; flat ribbing application; securing beginning stitches.

## Materials needed:

◆ ⅙ yard (.2m) of woven polyester/cotton terry or one hand towel (will make two mitts)

◆ 5″ (12.5cm) of polyester/cotton ribbing (will make two mitts)

*THE POLYESTER/COTTON BLEND ALLOWS THE FABRIC AND RIBBING TO DRY QUICKLY AFTER EACH USE.*

◆ Matching serger or all-purpose thread for serging

## Cutting directions:

■ Cut two 10″ by 6″ (25.5cm by 15cm) rectangles of the terry.

■ Cut one 8″ by 5″ (20.5cm by 12.5cm) rectangle of the ribbing, with the greatest stretch running lengthwise on the rectangle.

**SERGER SETTINGS:**

3- or 3/4-thread balanced stitch

**Stitch length:** Medium for seaming; long for ribbing application.

**Stitch width:** Wide

**Needle:** Size 11/75

## How-tos:

Serge-seam using ¼″ (6mm) allowances, just skimming the edges with the knives.

1 Place the terry rectangles right sides together and, using a saucer as a guide, round the corners on one short end.

2 Beginning at one square corner, serge-seam the sides and curved end, just skimming the edges with the knives. Stop approximately 4″ (10cm) from the other square corner. Raise the presser foot and needle, pull the fabric behind the needle, and chain off. (Fig. 5-29)

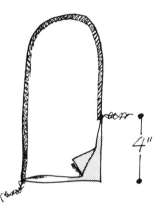

*Fig. 5-29 Leave a section unserged so the ribbing can be applied flat.*

*WHEN SERGING AROUND THE CURVES, WATCH THE KNIVES INSTEAD OF THE NEEDLE(S). SERGE SLOWLY TO GUIDE THE FABRIC ACCURATELY, HOLDING IT IN A STRAIGHT LINE IN FRONT OF THE PRESSER FOOT. (SEE FIG. 1-22)*

3 Fold the ribbing in half lengthwise, wrong sides together, and mark the center point on the long cut edges. Pin the ribbing to the right side of the mitt, aligning the marking with the mitt seamline. Adjust to a long stitch and the highest differential feed setting. Serge-seam the ribbing to the mitt, with the ribbing on top and stretching the ribbing to fit the fabric.

*Fig. 5-28 Enjoy bathing with this simple textured mitt.*

BE CAREFUL NOT TO HIT THE PINS
WITH THE KNIVES. WHEN THE
PRESSER FOOT REACHES A PIN,
REMOVE IT WHILE KEEPING THE
RIBBING STRETCHED AND
CONTINUE SERGING.

4 Secure the beginning
stitches when serging the
remaining unfinished edge
by first serging several
inches of thread chain.
Then, with right sides
together and the cut edges
matching, serge two stitches
onto the ribbing, beginning
at the folded edges.

5 Stop stitching with the
needle in the fabric and raise
the presser foot. Gently
stretch the thread chain out
in back of the presser foot,
smoothing the loops so the
chain is thinner.

6 Bring the chain around
under the presser foot
between the needle and
knives and lower the presser
foot. Slowly stitch over it for
about 1" (2.5cm). Move the
remaining thread chain to
the right to be trimmed by
the knives as you continue
serging. (See Fig. 2-16)

7 Continue serging, matching
the seamlines and lapping the
beginning stitches for about
½" (1.3cm). (Fig. 5-30)

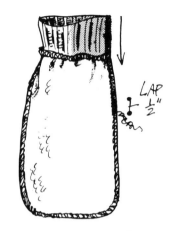

*Fig. 5-30 Neatly secure the
beginning stitches by machine at the
cuff edge before finishing the
remainder of the side seam.*

AS YOU LAP THE SERGING, BE
CAREFUL NOT TO CUT THE
BEGINNING STITCHES. WHEN
SERGING OVER THEM, MOVE THE
FABRIC SLIGHTLY TO THE LEFT OF
THE KNIVES.

8 Raise the needle and presser
foot, pull the fabric behind
the needle, and chain off.
Knot the thread chain
securely next to the fabric
edge and clip the excess.

# Notes

# 6 Painless Rolled Edges

By making a few adjustments to your machine's basic 3-thread stitch, you can neatly and attractively finish or seam fabric using a narrow rolled edge. This short, narrow stitch rolls the fabric edge to the underside. (See page 13)

Following the instructions in your owner's manual, adjust the stitch width, length, and tension. Change the needle plate and/or presser foot, or make any other required adjustments. Remember to use a sharp new needle, inserting it in the proper position.

ALWAYS TEST ON PROJECT SCRAPS (AND ON THE SAME NUMBER OF LAYERS YOU'LL BE SERGING) TO PERFECT THE STITCH BEFORE SEWING ANY GARMENT OR PROJECT.

Because of differences in both fabric weight and thread, adjustments often have to be made. Follow these basic guidelines:

- If the upper looper thread does not wrap the edge completely to the underside, tighten the lower looper-thread tension even more. (Fig. 6-1)

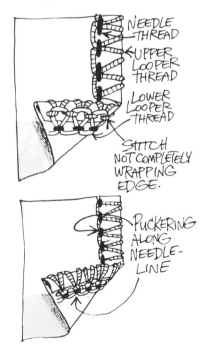

Fig. 6-1 *Perfect a rolled-edge stitch by tightening the lower looper-thread tension enough to wrap the upper looper thread completely around the edge. Loosen the needle-thread tension if the fabric puckers.*

- If the fabric puckers along the seamline, loosen the needle-thread tension slightly.

- For the cleanest rolled-edge finish, trim part of the seam allowance with the knives as you serge.

- If the stitches begin to pull away from the fabric edge, lengthen the stitch. Other helpful options are to widen the stitch slightly or loosen the lower looper tension.

- If you have problems with skipped stitches, try prewashing the fabric to remove any sizing.

- If tiny fibers poke out through the stitching, try widening the stitch so that the fabric wraps the edge completely or shorten the stitch for more thread coverage. (Woolly nylon thread will also give more thread coverage.)

Some serger models can also be adjusted for a 2-thread rolled edge (check your owner's manual). For this stitch, you will use the needle thread and one looper thread, tightening the needle-thread tension so the looper thread wraps the edge to the underside. On any project in this chapter, you may substitute the 2-thread rolled edge if you want an attractive lighter-weight option. (Fig. 6-2)

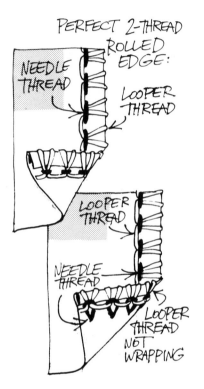

Fig. 6-2 *If the looper thread on a 2-thread rolled edge does not wrap completely to the underside, tighten the needle-thread tension.*

*FOR MORE INFORMATION ON ROLLED EDGES, REFER TO CHAPTER 14 IN* ABCS OF SERGING. *GARMENT APPLICATIONS FOR ROLLED EDGES ARE ALSO FEATURED THROUGHOUT* SERGED GARMENTS IN MINUTES, *INCLUDING THE CHART ON PAGE 113 THAT LISTS ALL OF THE EDGE-FINISHING OPTIONS.*

Fig. 6-3 *A rolled-edge finish outlines the reversed facing and hems.*

# RELAXED ROUND-NECK TOP

Decorative reversed hems and a matching reversed facing are featured on this easy lightweight top. (Fig. 6-3)

## SKILLS USED:

Rolled-edge finishing; rolled-edge seams; reversed facing and hems.

## Materials needed:

◆ Basic loose-fitting pullover top pattern with a faced scoop neckline, short sleeves, and dropped shoulders

- Lightweight woven fabric with no definite right and wrong side, such as a solid-color silky polyester or rayon, following the pattern yardage requirements

- Lightweight fusible interfacing, following the pattern yardage requirements (test on the project fabric before using)

- Matching serger or all-purpose thread for serging; matching all-purpose thread for the sewing machine

## Cutting directions:

- Make any necessary pattern alterations.

- Cut one front, one back, two sleeves, and two facing pieces from the fabric.

- Cut interfacing for the two facing pieces.

**SERGER SETTINGS:**

3-thread rolled-edge stitch

**Stitch length:** Short for finishing; medium for seaming

**Stitch width:** Narrow

**Needle:** Size 11/75

## How-tos:

Serge-seam with the needle on the seamline, trimming any excess seam allowances with the knives. Test the rolled-edge stitch on project fabric scraps—you will use it for all of the seaming and finishing in this project. Test by serging on both one and two layers as well as on interfaced fabric scraps.

WHEN ROLLED-EDGE SEAMING, YOU MAY NEED TO WIDEN THE STITCH TO ALLOW THE BULK OF THE TWO FABRIC EDGES TO ROLL ENTIRELY TO THE UNDERSIDE. BE CAREFUL NOT TO STRETCH THE LIGHTWEIGHT FABRIC WHEN SERGING BECAUSE IT CAN RUFFLE. IF IT DOES, LENGTHEN THE STITCH SLIGHTLY. IF THE SEAM PUCKERS ON THE LIGHT-WEIGHT FABRIC, ADJUST THE DIFFERENTIAL FEED TO ITS LOWEST SETTING AND USE TAUT SERGING. (SEE FIG. 1-18)

1 Serge-seam the garment shoulders, right sides together.

2 Fuse the interfacing to the wrong side of the front and back facings, then serge-seam the facings, right sides together, at the shoulders.

3 Finish the outer facing edge from the right side, lapping the serging ½". Raise the needle and the presser foot, pull the fabric behind the needle, and chain off.

BE CAREFUL NOT TO CUT THE BEGINNING STITCHES AS YOU SERGE OVER THEM BY MOVING THE EDGE SLIGHTLY AWAY FROM THE KNIVES.

4 Place the right side of the facing against the wrong side of the neckline edge, matching the seamlines. Position the seam allowances in opposite directions. Seam the neckline edge, lapping the stitching for ½". Carefully press the facing to the right side, tuck the thread-chain end under the outer facing edge and top-stitch the outer facing edge to the garment along the serged needleline. Stitch-in-the-ditch at the shoulder seams. (Fig. 6-4)

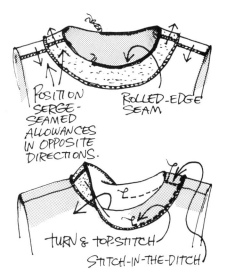

Fig. 6-4 Feature the neckline facing on the right side of the garment.

5 From the wrong side of the fabric, finish the lower edges of both sleeves. Press the hem allowances to the right side.

6 Seam the sleeves to the garment, right sides together, with the garment on top.

7 Open out the sleeve hem allowances and match the side/sleeve-underarm edges on one side, right sides together. Seam from the lower edge to the bottom of the sleeve. (Fig. 6-5)

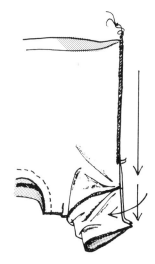

Fig. 6-5 Seam one side and underarm before finishing the lower edge.

ADJUST THE FABRIC SO THE
EDGES AND SHOULDER SEAMS
MEET EXACTLY. PULL THE EDGE
STRAIGHT IN FRONT OF THE
PRESSER FOOT AS YOU REACH
THE UNDERARM CORNER.

8 From the wrong side, finish
the lower edge, serging
slowly over the seamline to
ensure even stitching.

9 Match the side/sleeve-
underarm edges, right sides
together, on the opposite
side. Seam from the lower
edge to the bottom of the
sleeve.

10 Turn the lower and sleeve
hems to the right side and
top-stitch them in place,
tucking the excess thread-
chain ends under the
hems. (Fig. 6-6)

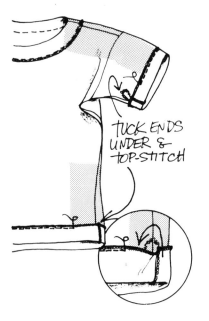

TUCK ENDS
UNDER &
TOP-STITCH

*Fig. 6-6 Secure the ends of the
serging by tucking the thread chains
under the hems before top-stitching.*

# WIDE-LEGGED POCKETED SHORTS

Use this simple method to
construct any basic pull-on
shorts, pants, or split skirt.
Rolled-edge seaming throughout gives a neat finish when the
reversed hems are turned to the
right side. (Fig. 6-7)

## SKILLS USED:

Rolled-edge seams; serging
curves; inseam pockets; serged,
turned, and top-stitched waistline casing; reversed elastic
hems.

## *Materials needed:*

◆ Basic wide-legged pull-on
shorts pattern with inseam
pockets and a fold-down
elastic waistband casing

◆ Lightweight woven fabric
with no definite right and
wrong side, such as a solid-
color silky polyester or
rayon, following the pattern
yardage requirements

◆ Waistband elastic, the length
specified on the pattern in
the width you prefer

*Fig. 6-7 Coordinate the shorts with
the round-neck top by reversing the
hems to match.*

◆ Matching serger or all-
purpose thread for serging;
matching all-purpose thread
for the sewing machine

## *Cutting directions:*

■ Make any necessary pattern
alterations.

■ If the elastic width is
different than specified in
the pattern requirements,
adjust both the front and
back pattern pieces for a
waistline casing double the
elastic width plus ½"
(1.3cm).

■ Check to be sure the
finished waistline
measurement is large
enough to pull over your
hips. Add more width to the
front and back waistline
edges if necessary.

■ Cut out the front and back
pieces.

**SERGER SETTINGS:**

3-thread rolled-edge stitch

**Stitch length:** Short for finishing; medium for seaming

**Stitch width:** Narrow

**Needle:** Size 11/75

## How-tos:

Serge-seam with the needle on the seamline, trimming any excess seam allowances with the knives. Test the rolled-edge stitch by serging on both one and two layers of project fabric scraps—you will use it for all of the seaming and finishing in this project.

*WIDEN THE STITCH IF THE EDGES ARE NOT ROLLING TO THE UNDERSIDE. IF THE SEAM RUFFLES, LENGTHEN THE STITCH SLIGHTLY. IF THE SEAM PUCKERS, ADJUST THE DIFFERENTIAL FEED TO ITS LOWEST SETTING AND USE TAUT SERGING. (SEE FIG. 1-18)*

*1* With right sides together and beginning at the lower edge, serge the front and back sections together at the inseams.

*HOLD THE THREAD CHAIN TAUT WHEN BEGINNING TO SERGE TO PREVENT THE SEAMS FROM PULLING UP ON THE LIGHTWEIGHT FABRIC.*

*2* Place the joined pieces right sides together at the crotch and seam, holding the curved area in a straight line in front of the presser foot as you serge over it. Reinforce the curve by straight-stitching along the serged needleline. (Fig. 6-8)

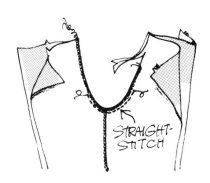

*Fig. 6-8 Reinforce the curved crotch area after seaming the two sides together.*

*3* Finish the lower edges from the wrong side and press the hem allowances to the right side.

*IF YOU ARE UNSURE OF THE FIT AT THIS POINT, PIN THE SIDE SEAMS TOGETHER, TRY ON THE SHORTS, AND MAKE ANY NECESSARY ADJUSTMENTS BEFORE PROCEEDING WITH STEP 4.*

*4* With right sides together, seam the pocket pieces to the seam allowances on both sides, front and back. On one side, match the cut edges and pocket seam, folding the pocket out, and straight-stitch from the upper edge to the top of the pocket opening and back-stitch to secure. At the lower pocket edge, back-stitch and straight-stitch on the seam-line for 3″ to 4″. (Fig. 6-9)

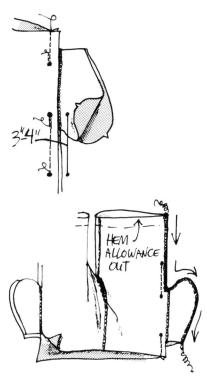

*Fig. 6-9 Quickly apply inseam pockets in shorts, pants, or skirts.*

*5* Pin the side and outer pocket edges parallel to the seamline about ¹/₂″ (1.3cm) left of it, folding the hem allowance out flat. Beginning at the lower edge, seam up the side and around the pocket.

*WHEN YOU REACH THE LOWER POCKET EDGE, SERGE AT AN ANGLE OFF THE SIDE SEAM ONTO THE POCKET, PULLING THE CURVE OUT STRAIGHT IN FRONT OF THE PRESSER FOOT AS YOU SERGE OVER IT. THEN SERGE AROUND THE REMAINDER OF THE OUTER POCKET EDGES, CONTINUING TO PULL THE CURVED AREA STRAIGHT IN FRONT OF THE FOOT.*

6 Finish the waistline edge from the right side.

7 Following the instructions in steps 4 and 5, seam the other side and outer pocket edge.

8 Press the pockets toward the front. Fold the waistline casing to the wrong side and top-stitch it in place, leaving an opening for threading the elastic.

9 Thread the elastic through the casing, adjust it to a comfortable fit, lap the ends ½", and zigzag them together. Then straight-stitch the opening closed.

*PULL THE ELASTIC AND FABRIC OUT TO ITS MAXIMUM WIDTH AND THEN RELEASE IT TO DISTRIBUTE THE GATHERS EVENLY. FROM THE RIGHT SIDE, STITCH-IN-THE-DITCH OF THE SEAMLINES TO SECURE THE ELASTIC AND PREVENT IT FROM ROLLING IN THE CASING.*

10 Turn up the hem allowances to the right side and top-stitch them in place along the serged needlelines, tucking the thread chain ends underneath before stitching.

# STRETCHABLE HAIR RING

Twist this quick-serged fabric-covered elastic ornament around your hair to keep it neatly in place and add a splash of color. (Fig. 6-10)

**SKILLS USED:**

Rolled-edge seaming; serging in a circle.

## Materials needed:

◆ ⅙ yard (.2m) of woven or knit fabric, such as silky polyester, metallic, or interlock

◆ 10" (25.5cm) of ⅜"-wide (1cm) or narrower elastic

◆ Matching serger or all-purpose thread for serging

*Fig. 6-10 Use the rolled-edge stitch to decoratively seam a fashionable hair ornament.*

## Cutting directions:

Cut a 27" by 6" (68.5cm by 15cm) strip of fabric.

*FOR LIGHTWEIGHT FABRIC, YOU CAN CUT A LONGER STRIP—UP TO 45" (114CM)—FOR MORE FULLNESS. FOR HEAVIER FABRIC, SUCH AS INTERLOCK, THE STRIP SHOULD BE SHORTER.*

**SERGER SETTINGS:**

3-thread rolled-edge stitch

**Stitch length:** Short

**Stitch width:** Narrow

**Needle:** Size 11/75

## How-tos:

1 Seam the short ends of the strip, right sides together.

2 Tie the elastic into a circle, and knot securely. Clip the ends to approximately 1" (2.5cm).

TIE THE ELASTIC CIRCLE SMALLER IF YOU PREFER TO WEAR THE RING SINGLE-LAYER WITHOUT TWISTING IT AROUND YOUR HAIR A SECOND TIME.

3 Fold the fabric around the elastic circle, wrong sides together, matching the edges and seamline. Beginning close to the seamline, seam the edges together, pulling the fabric straight as you serge over it. Lap the beginning serging for approximately ½" (1.3cm), being careful not to cut the previous stitches. Raise the needle and presser foot, pull the fabric behind the needle, and chain off. (Fig. 6-11)

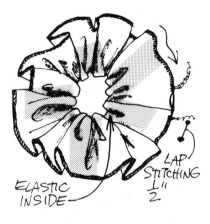

*Fig. 6-11 Fold the fabric circle around the elastic circle and serge the outer edges together.*

# CLOVERLEAF-BOW PICTURE HANGER

You can easily make ribbon on your serger by quickly serging the edges of fabric strips. This clever hanger for a small picture is just one of many possible uses for serged ribbon. (Fig. 6-12)

**SKILLS USED:**
Rolled-edge finishing.

*Fig. 6-12 Turn a small painting into a major decorating statement by adding a simple serge-finished bow.*

## Materials needed:

◆ ½ yard (.5m) of 45"-wide (114cm) woven fabric, such as taffeta

◆ ⅝ yard (.6m) of regular paper-backed fusible web

◆ Matching serger or all-purpose thread for serging

◆ Air-erasable marker

◆ Floral or beading wire (available in craft stores)

◆ Seam sealant

## Cutting directions:

- Cut four 4″ by 18″ (10cm by 46cm) strips from the fusible web.

- Using the marker, draw the grid on the back of the fabric. (Fig. 6-13)

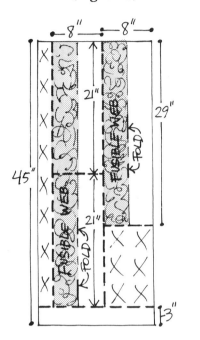

Fig. 6-13 *After fusing the web in the positions indicated, cut out the four sections on the dotted lines.*

- Following the manufacturer's instructions, fuse the web strips to the fabric as illustrated, butting the ends to piece the strips as necessary.

- Cut out the hanger sections on the dotted lines.

### SERGER SETTINGS:

3-thread rolled-edge stitch

**Stitch length:** Short

**Stitch width:** Narrow

**Needle:** Size 11/75

## How-tos:

Test the rolled-edge stitch by serging on two fused and unfused layers of the project fabric.

1  Remove the fusible-web paper backing on the three 8″-wide sections. Fold the strips wrong sides together, sandwiching the fusible web in between. Fuse the layers together.

2  Serge-seam a short end of one 21″ section to a short end of the 29″ section. Cut the unseamed ends diagonally.

3  Finish all the edges of both fused strips, using the rolled-edge stitch. (Fig. 6-14)

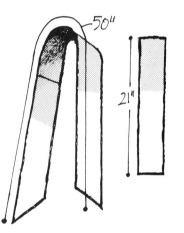

Fig. 6-14 *Finish the edges of the fused strips with a rolled-edge stitch.*

**BECAUSE OF THE FUSIBLE WEB, YOU MAY NEED TO WIDEN THE STITCH SO THE EDGES CAN ROLL COMPLETELY TO THE UNDERSIDE.**

4  Press the 3″-wide unfused strip in half lengthwise, wrong sides together. Serge-finish both long edges, then the short ends.

**BEFORE SERGING THE UNFUSED STRIP, TEST THE ROLLED-EDGE STITCH AGAIN. YOU MAY NEED TO NARROW THE STITCH TO PERFECT IT.**

5  Dab the corners of all three strips with seam sealant and clip the excess thread when dry.

6  Fold the remaining 21″ strip into a circle, lapping the ends 2″ in the center. Wrap the floral wire around the center to form a bow. (Fig. 6-15)

Fig. 6-15 *Wire the two sections together before finishing the hanger in step 8.*

7 Fold the longer fused strip in half crosswise with the seam on the back side. Twist the ribbon 4" from the top, reversing the top section. Position the bow on top of the twisted area and join the two pieces with the wire tails.

8 Crisscross the unfused strip around the center of the bow. Pull the ends tightly together on the back side and hand-stitch them in place, trimming the excess.

9 To use the bow, first mount the picture on the wall using picture wire and a hook. Then remove the picture and tack the streamers to the back of the frame. Rehang the picture and tack the bow to the wall above it.

## CRAZY NO-TIE SCARF

Quickly roll the edges of this uniquely shaped scarf. Pull any corner through the loop on the long narrow end for a variety of wearing options. (Fig. 6-16)

**SKILLS USED:**

Rolled-edge finishing; serging curves.

*Fig. 6-16 Add new interest to your wardrobe with a versatile no-tie scarf.*

### Materials needed:

◆ ⁷⁄₈ yard (.8m) of lightweight woven silk, silky polyester, or rayon fabric with no definite right or wrong side (will make two scarves or one double-layer scarf)

*IF YOU WANT TO GIVE THE SCARF MORE BODY OR IF THE FABRIC HAS A DEFINITE RIGHT AND WRONG SIDE, CUT TWO SCARF PIECES, PLACE THEM WRONG SIDES TOGETHER, AND TREAT THEM AS ONE LAYER.*

- Matching serger or all-purpose thread for serging; matching all-purpose thread for the sewing machine

- Seam sealant

## Cutting directions:

- Cut the scarf following the pattern. (Fig. 6-17)

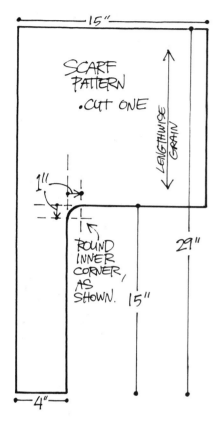

Fig. 6-17 *Cut out two scarves with the fabric folded lengthwise for more weight or if the fabric has a definite right and wrong side.*

**SERGER SETTINGS:**

3-thread rolled-edge stitch

**Stitch length:** Medium

**Stitch width:** Narrow

**Needle:** Size 11/75

## How-tos:

1 After testing the rolled-edge stitch, serge-finish the lengthwise scarf edges from the right side, holding the thread chain taut as you begin serging. (Fig. 6-18)

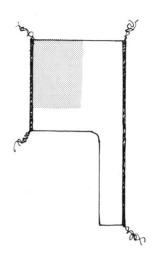

Fig. 6-18 *Finish the lengthwise edges first.*

2 Serge-finish both straight crosswise edges.

3 Beginning at the narrow end, serge-finish the remaining edge. To easily serge the curved area, stop when the knives are about 1/2″ (1.3cm) from the corner, with the needle in the down position. Pull the curve into a straight line as you serge over it and continue serging the edge.

4 Secure the ends with a dab of seam sealant on each corner and clip the excess thread when dry.

APPLY THE SEAM SEALANT LIGHTLY WITH A PIN OR TOOTHPICK TO AVOID STAINING THE FABRIC.

5 Fold under 2 1/2″ (6.5cm) on the long narrow end and top-stitch it in place, forming a loop. Pull one of the opposite corners through the loop to secure the scarf around your neck. (Fig. 6-19)

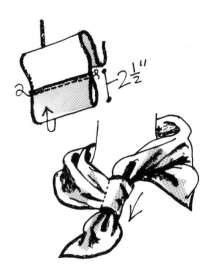

Fig. 6-19 *Sew a loop at the long narrow end and thread a corner of the scarf through it after wrapping it around your neck.*

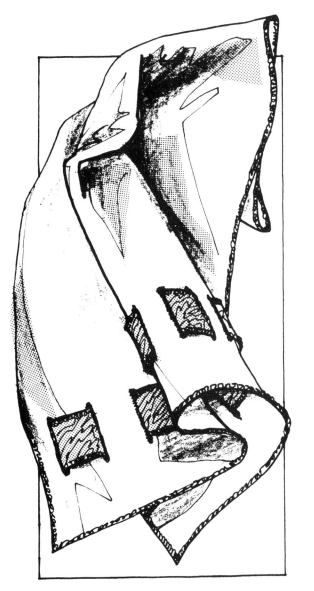

# WOVEN ACCENT NAPKINS

Weave a serge-finished strip through buttonholes to add an interesting accent to these special luncheon-size napkins. Increase the dimensions as desired for larger dinner napkins. (Fig. 6-20)

### SKILLS USED:

Rolled-edge finishing; sewing buttonholes.

*Fig. 6-20 Embellish simple rolled-edge napkins with a contrasting woven strip.*

## Materials needed:

- ◆ ⁷/₈″ yard (.8m) of 45″-wide (114cm) medium-weight woven fabric for the napkins (will make six)

- ◆ ¹/₈″ yard (.1m) of contrasting fabric for the woven strips (the fabric can be lighter-weight)

- ◆ Matching serger or all-purpose thread for serging; matching all-purpose thread for the sewing machine

- ◆ Air-erasable marker

- ◆ Seam sealant

## Cutting directions:

- ■ Prewash the fabric before cutting to remove any sizing. Stiff sizing will often prevent the fabric edge from rolling or may cause skipped stitches.

- ■ Cut a 15″ (38cm) square for each napkin.

- ■ Cut a 16″ (40.5cm) by 1¹/₈″ (2.8cm) strip of the contrasting fabric for each napkin.

*FOR FASTEST CUTTING, SQUARE THE FABRIC ON A RULED CUTTING MAT AND CUT BOTH THE NAPKINS AND STRIPS WITH A ROTARY CUTTER.*

SERGER SETTINGS:

3-thread rolled-edge stitch

**Stitch length:** Short

**Stitch width:** Narrow

**Needle:** Size 11/75

## How-tos:

When serge-finishing, just skim the fabric edges with the knives. Test the rolled-edge stitch on a single layer of the project fabric. If the fabric does not roll completely, widen the stitch, if this is possible on your serger model.

*IF YOU STILL HAVE DIFFICULTY GETTING THE EDGE TO ROLL, SWITCH TO LIGHTWEIGHT MONOFILAMENT NYLON THREAD IN THE LOWER LOOPER AND LOOSEN THAT TENSION SLIGHTLY. THE STRENGTH OF THE NYLON THREAD CAN HELP PERFECT ANY ROLLED EDGE.*

1 Serge-finish both long edges of each strip.

2 Using the marker, draw 1"-long (2.5cm) buttonhole placements on each napkin. Position them vertically 2" (5cm) above one cut edge, 1" (2.5cm) apart, and 1" (2.5cm) from both sides. (Fig. 6-21)

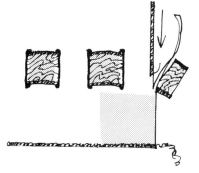

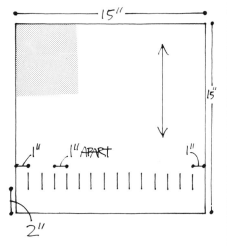

*Fig. 6-21 Mark the buttonhole positions on one napkin edge, parallel to the lengthwise grain.*

*Fig. 6-22 Let the knives trim off the excess ends of the strip as you serge over them.*

3 Adjust your sewing machine for making buttonholes and sew one buttonhole on each marked line. Using a pin or toothpick, dab seam sealant between the stitching lines on each buttonhole.

4 Allow the seam sealant to dry, then cut the buttonholes open.

5 Beginning from the wrong side, weave the strip through the buttonholes, with both right side up, allowing ½" (1.3cm) to extend on both ends.

6 Serge-finish the upper and lower edges of the napkin.

7 Serge-finish both sides of the napkin, catching the strip ends in the serging. (Fig. 6-22)

8 Dab seam sealant on each corner and clip the excess thread when dry.

# VICTORIAN NOSEGAY ORNAMENT

Add a touch of nostalgia to your holiday decorating with this lovely ornament. Use one as a pretty accent on a gift box, too. (Fig. 6-23)

## SKILLS USED:

Lettuced, rolled edge; differential-feed gathering.

*Fig. 6-23 For a show-stopping effect, decorate an entire tree or wreath with nosegays.*

## Materials needed:

- One yard (.95m) of light-weight lace or tulle fabric
- Matching or coordinating serger or all-purpose thread for serging
- One small floral spray
- 18″ (46cm) of ³⁄₈″-wide (1cm) ribbon
- Green floral tape (available in craft stores)

## Cutting directions:

- Fold the fabric diagonally and cut an 8″-wide (20.5cm) bias strip the length of the bias fold.

**SERGER SETTINGS:**

3-thread rolled-edge stitch

**Stitch length:** Short

**Stitch width:** Narrow

**Needle:** Size 11/75

## How-tos:

1 Fold the strip in half length-wise, wrong sides together. Begin lettucing the long folded edge by anchoring a few stitches into the fabric. Adjust the differential feed to the lowest setting, hold the thread chain behind the presser foot and the fabric edge in front, and begin serging.

2 Continue serging the length of the edge, stretching evenly in front of and behind the presser foot. Be careful not to pull the fabric more in either direction or the needle could break. (Fig. 6-24)

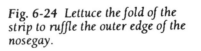

Fig. 6-24 *Lettuce the fold of the strip to ruffle the outer edge of the nosegay.*

3 Adjust the serger to a long, wide, balanced stitch and the differential feed to its highest setting. If your model doesn't have differential feed, tighten the needle-thread tension slightly. Beginning at the finished edge, serge-gather the three unfinished edges, rounding the corners by trimming with the knives. (Fig. 6-25)

4 Smooth out the thread chain on one end. Find the shortest thread in the chain (the needle thread) and gently pull it to tightly gather half the rosette. Repeat for the other end of the rosette. (Fig. 6-26)

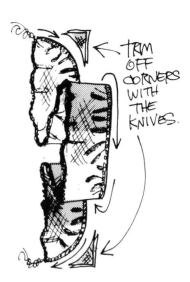

Fig. 6-25 *Serge-gather the remaining edges using a long wide balanced stitch and the highest differential-feed setting.*

Fig. 6-26 *Pull the needle thread from both ends to gather the strip tightly before wrapping it around the floral spray.*

5 Wrap the rosette tightly around the spray and knot it with the thread-chain ends. Hand-stitch the bottom together around the stems of the spray, then tightly wrap the thread around the lower ¾" (2cm) of fabric. (Fig. 6-27)

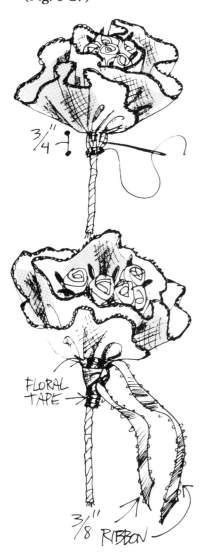

Fig. 6-27 Hand-stitch the bottom securely and wrap the lower edge of the nosegay before finishing with floral tape and tying on the ribbon.

6 Cover the wrapped area and stems with the floral tape, then tie and hand-stitch the center of the ribbon around the bottom of the nosegay and trim the ends diagonally.

# ROUND RUFFLED TABLE TOPPER

Top a longer tablecloth with this ruffle-trimmed round for a soft layered effect. (Fig. 6-28)

### SKILLS USED:

Rolled-edge finishing; rolled-edge seams; differential-feed gathering; serged seams; serging curves.

## Materials needed:

- 1⅞ yard (1.8m) of 45"-wide (114cm) lightweight woven fabric, such as gingham or batiste

- Matching serger or all-purpose thread for serging

- Air-erasable marker

- Seam sealant

Fig. 6-28 Put your serging skills to work on a round table cover.

## Cutting directions:

- Cut a 45" (114cm) square from the fabric for the table topper.

- Cut five 45" by 4" (114cm by 10cm) strips from the fabric for the ruffle.

- Fold the square in half and then in half again. Then fold once more diagonally. Using a tape measure and the marker, pivot from the folded corner point and draw a curved line. Cut on the marked line to form a round piece. (Fig. 6-29)

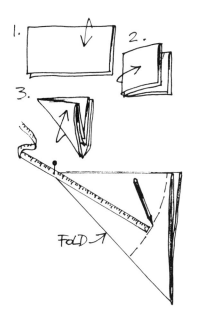

Fig. 6-29 *Pivot the measuring tape from the corner point to mark the circle evenly.*

## SERGER SETTINGS:

3-thread rolled-edge stitch

**Stitch length:** Short

**Stitch width:** Narrow

**Needle:** Size 11/75

## How-tos:

Serge-seam using ¼" (6mm) allowances, trimming if necessary.

1 Using the rolled edge, finish the edges of the table topper from the right side, lapping the beginning stitches ½" (1.3cm). Dab seam sealant on the end and clip the excess thread when dry.

2 Serge-seam the short ends of the strips right sides together to form one long strip.

3 From the right side of the long strip, serge-finish one short end and one long edge.

4 Adjust the serger to a long, medium-width, balanced stitch and the differential feed to the highest setting. If your model doesn't have differential feed, tighten the needle tension slightly. Serge-gather the long unfinished edge.

*TO CREATE MORE GATHERS, EASE-PLUS BY GENTLY FORCE-FEEDING THE FABRIC UNDER THE FRONT OF THE PRESSER FOOT AND HOLDING IT AS IT EXITS OUT THE BACK. (SEE FIG. 1-17)*

5 Pin the ruffle, right sides together, to the outside edges of the table topper, allowing a 3" (7.5cm) overlap. Trim the ruffle to this line and temporarily unpin the lap. (Fig. 6-30)

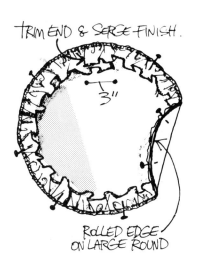

Fig. 6-30 *Pin the ruffle to the circle, adjusting the gathers evenly.*

6 Adjust to a narrow, medium-length, balanced stitch with no differential feed. Finish the unfinished ruffle end and repin the lap back into position.

7 Raise the presser foot and needle and insert the table topper and ruffle, with the ruffle on top. Lower the needle and presser foot and serge-seam, lapping the beginning stitches ½" (1.3cm) and being careful not to cut them with the knives. Dab seam sealant on the ends and clip the excess thread when dry.

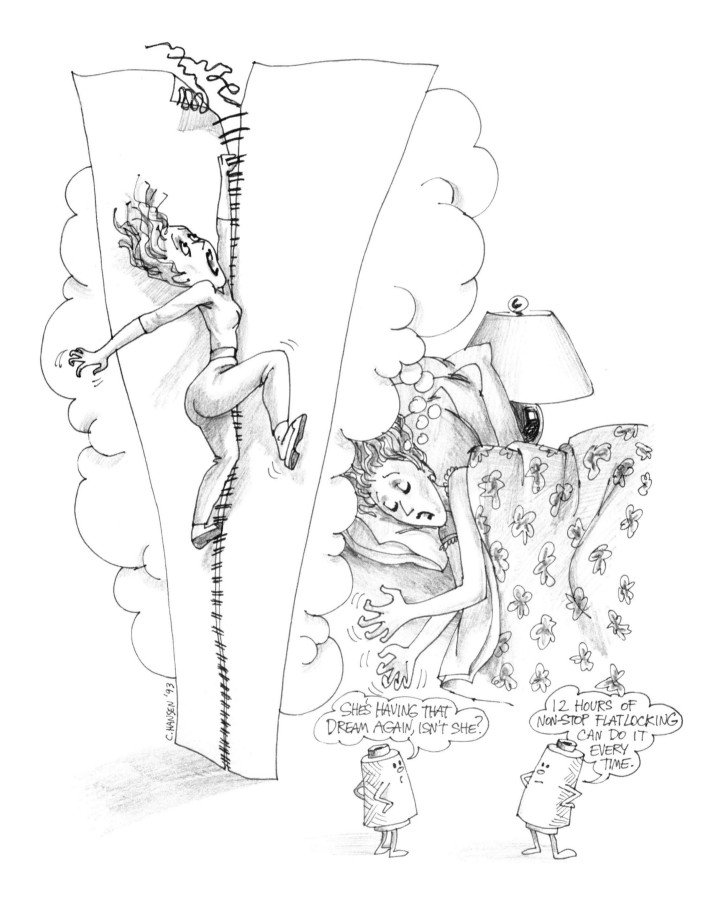

# 7 Focus On Flatlocking

By changing tensions you can adjust any serger for flatlocking, a useful serging option. Flatlocking is ideal for decoratively serging over folds and for bulk-free seaming. The flatlock stitch will show on both sides of the fabric. (See page 14)

With few exceptions, all serger models have a 3-thread stitch and can be adjusted for 3-thread flatlocking. Use a wide, short to medium-length balanced stitch and loosen the needle-thread tension almost completely. (See Fig. 1-30) Tighten the lower looper-thread tension, but (in most cases) don't change the upper looper-thread tension.

Serge along a fold or edge, letting the stitches hang halfway off the fabric. Then gently pull the fabric and stitching flat. (Fig. 7-1)

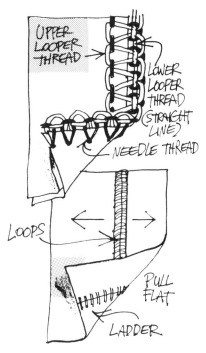

Fig. 7-1 Flatlock with the stitches hanging halfway off the edge. The fabric will pull flat underneath the stitches. When flatlock-seaming, the edges will meet under the center of the stitching.

IF THE FLATLOCK STITCHES AREN'T FORMING, TRY LOOSENING THE LOWER LOOPER-THREAD TENSION SLIGHTLY.

Some serger models have a 2-thread overedge stitch that can be used for flatlocking with few or no tension adjustments because the stitch does not lock at the seamline. The 2-thread flatlock is less bulky, uses less thread, and stretches even more than a 3-thread flatlock. After serging an edge or fold with a wide, short to medium-length, balanced 2-thread overedge stitch, simply pull the fabric and stitching flat. (Fig. 7-2)

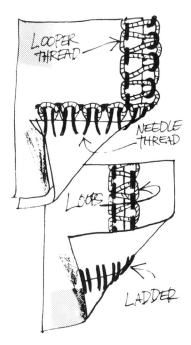

Fig. 7-2 Use a 2-thread overlock stitch, if available on your serger model, for flatlocking with few or no tension adjustments.

Always use a sharp new needle and test the stitch on scraps of the project fabric. Review Chapter 13 in *ABCs of Serging* for flatlocking specifics and remember these fundamentals:

- For any flatlocked seaming, you'll be guiding the fabric away from the knives so the stitches can hang off the edge. Because of this, the knives won't be cutting the fabric, so you must pretrim any allowances that are wider than half the stitch width.

*FOR OPTIONAL TYPES OF FLAT-LOCK SEAMING, SEE PAGE 24 IN SERGED GARMENTS IN MINUTES.*

- Use an optional blindhem foot, if one is available for your model, to guide the fabric edge or fold accurately.

- Most flatlocking, especially when serging over folds, is easier and more accurate when done in a straight line. Curves can be difficult.

- Flatlock with wrong sides together to position the loops on the right side of the fabric. Put the right sides together if you want the ladder stitch on the right side.

- For best results, flatlock on stable, ravel-free fabrics or finish the edges before flatlocking over them.

- When 3-thread flatlocking with decorative thread, use it in the upper looper when the loops will be on the right side. Use decorative thread in the needle when the ladder stitches will be on the right side, but remember that the thread must be fine enough to fit through the needle eye.

- When serging across two rows of flatlocked stitching, secure the first end by pulling the thread-chain toward the fabric, away from the edge, before serging over it and catching the thread chain in the stitching. (Always pull the thread chain to the wrong side of the fabric.) Then trim the excess. For extra durability, knot the thread-chain end or use seam sealant before trimming. (Fig. 7-3)

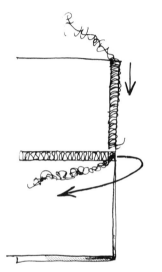

*Fig. 7-3 Secure a flatlocking thread-chain end in the crossing stitches to prevent it from unraveling.*

# HOODED POLAR-FLEECE PULLOVER

Avoid bulky seams on this stable and heavy knit fabric by flatlocking them for a durable option. The looped side of the stitch adds a sporty look to the garment. (Fig. 7-4)

### SKILLS USED:

Flatlocked seams; serging curves; sewing buttonholes; serged, turned, and top-stitched hems and hem casing.

## *Materials needed:*

- Basic loose-fitting pullover top with a hood, long sleeves, dropped shoulders, and hems at the lower and sleeve edges—designed for polar fleece or heavier stretch knits

*YOU MAY USE A PATTERN CALLING FOR RIBBING AT THE SLEEVES AND LOWER EDGE AND MAKE MINOR ADJUSTMENTS TO IT (SEE THE CUTTING DIRECTIONS).*

- Medium-weight polar fleece fabric, following the pattern yardage requirements

- Matching or contrasting serger or all-purpose thread for serging; matching all-purpose thread for the sewing machine

- Cording for the hood, following the pattern yardage requirements

- Air-erasable marker

Fig. 7-4 Use flatlocking for bulk-free yet sturdy seaming.

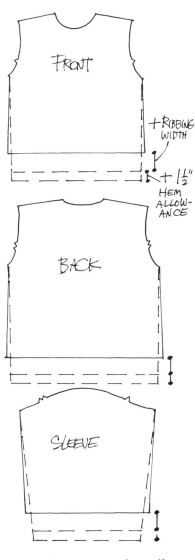

Fig. 7-5 Alter a pattern that calls for ribbing by tapering in slightly and adding the ribbing width plus a hem allowance to the lower edges.

## Cutting directions:

- Check the finished length on the back of the pattern envelope and make any necessary alterations on both the front and back pattern pieces. Check the sleeve length by pinning the front, back, and sleeve pattern pieces together and holding them over your shoulder. Bend your arm slightly for the most accurate measurement. Remember to allow for a sleeve hem allowance.

IF THE PATTERN CALLS FOR RIBBING AT THE SLEEVES AND LOWER EDGE, ADD THE WIDTH OF THE FINISHED RIBBING PLUS 1 1/2" (4CM) FOR A HEM ALLOWANCE TO THE LOWER SLEEVE, FRONT, AND BACK EDGES. BEFORE ADDING THE WIDTH, YOU MAY WANT TO TAPER THE SLEEVE AND TOP PATTERN PIECES SLIGHTLY, BUT REMEMBER TO ALLOW FOR THE BULK OF THE POLAR FLEECE. CUT THE HEM ALLOWANCE STRAIGHT DOWN, WITHOUT TAPERING IT. (FIG. 7-5)

- Cut one front, one back, two sleeves, and the hood from the polar fleece.

- Trim away all seam allowances (but not the hem allowances). Transfer all the pattern markings to the wrong side of the fabric, using the marker.

SERGER SETTINGS:

3-thread flatlock stitch

**Stitch length:** Medium

**Stitch width:** Wide

**Needle:** Size 14/90

### How-tos:

Flatlock with wrong sides together so the loops will show on the right side of the fabric. Allow several inches of thread chain to extend at the beginning and end of each seam to prevent it from pulling out during construction.

1 From the right side of the fabric, serge-finish the lower edges of the sleeves, front, and back, and the outer edges of the hood pieces without letting the stitches hang off the edge. If the hood opening is faced, serge-finish the inner facing edges.

*IT IS NOT NECESSARY TO FINISH THE EDGES OF KNIT POLAR FLEECE FABRIC. THE SERGING WILL PROVIDE NEATNESS AND DURABILITY.*

2 Adjust for the flatlock stitch and test on scraps of the polar fleece. With wrong sides together, flatlock-seam the shoulders. Pull the stitching flat, but do not trim the thread chains. (Fig. 7-6)

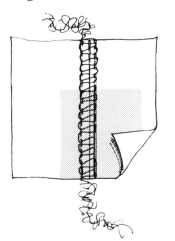

*Fig. 7-6 Flatlock the seams wrong sides together so the looped stitches show on the right side.*

*WHEN YOU TEST THE FLAT-LOCKING SEAMING, YOU MAY NEED TO LOOSEN THE UPPER LOOPER TENSION SLIGHTLY. MOVE THE FABRIC EDGES AWAY FROM THE KNIVES SO THE STITCH WILL PULL COMPLETELY FLAT.*

3 Use your sewing machine to make the buttonholes in the hood.

4 With wrong sides together, flatlock-seam the hood pieces (and the facing pieces if they're included in the pattern) and pull the stitching flat. With wrong sides together, flatlock the hood facing (if one is included) to the hood, but do not pull the seam flat.

*WHEN FLATLOCK-SEAMING THE CURVES, PULL THE FABRIC STRAIGHT IN FRONT OF THE PRESSER FOOT AND SERGE SLOWLY, ALLOWING THE STITCHES TO HANG OFF THE EDGE.*

5 Fold the hood hem (if no facing is included) to the wrong side. Top-stitch the hood edge to form a casing for the cording.

6 With wrong sides together and matching the markings, flatlock-seam the hood to the neckline, serging slowly and pulling the thread chains to the underside before you serge over them. Remember to pull the fabric straight in front of the presser foot when serging the curves. Be sure to catch all layers at the center-front neckline. Knot the thread chain close to the stitching and clip the excess.

*WHEN SERGING SEVERAL LAYERS OF THE POLAR FLEECE, YOU MAY NEED TO LOOSEN THE UPPER LOOPER TENSION ALSO TO CATCH ALL LAYERS AND TO BE ABLE TO PULL THE STITCHING FLAT.*

7 Pull the thread chain of the shoulder seam to the wrong side, away from the knives. With wrong sides together and the garment on top, flatlock the sleeves to the top and pull the stitching flat. Secure the thread chain, following directions in step 6. Lightly press the hems to the wrong side at the sleeve lower edges, then open them flat.

8 With wrong sides together, flatlock-seam the side/ sleeve seams, matching the underarm seams and pulling the thread chains away from the knives on both the upper and under sides to catch them in the seam. Pull the stitching flat.

9 Lightly press the hem to the wrong side at the lower edge. Tuck the thread chains into the sleeve and lower edge hems and top-stitch the hems in place. Thread the cording into the casing on the hood.

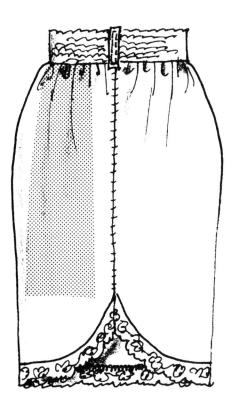

## LACE-TRIMMED HALF-SLIP

Quickly and easily flatlock-seam a nifty half-slip, cut to your measurements and featuring a curved slit. (Fig. 7-7)

**SKILLS USED:**

Flatlocked seams; serging curves.

## Materials needed:

◆ Nylon tricot fabric, equal to the desired finished length of the slip

◆ ³/₄″-wide (2cm) or wider matching or contrasting stretch lace with one flat side, equal to your waist measurement

◆ Matching or contrasting flat lace with one straight edge, equal to the total measurement of the slip's lower and slit edges plus 5″ (12.5cm)

*Fig. 7-7 Color-coordinate the stretch lace for the waistband and the flat lace for the trim.*

*USE THE SAME COLOR FOR BOTH LACES SO THAT THE SLIP WILL LOOK COORDINATED.*

◆ 6″ (15cm) of ³/₈″-wide (1cm) satin ribbon to match the slip fabric

◆ Matching medium-weight rayon thread or embroidery thread for serging; matching all-purpose thread for the sewing machine

◆ Seam sealant

## Cutting directions:

■ From the tricot, cut one rectangle 4″ (10cm) larger than the hip measurement by the finished length of the slip (from the waistline to the bottom edge) minus the width of the flat, nonstretch lace. Cut with the greatest stretch going around the body. (Fig. 7-8)

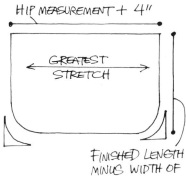

*Fig. 7-8 Round the lower corners sharply enough so the slip won't show beneath a skirt slit.*

■ Round the two lower corners of the rectangle to form the curved slit. Make a gradual curve 10″ to 12″ deep and angle it out enough so that the slip corners won't show beneath a skirt slit.

■ Wrap the stretch lace around your waistline comfortably and cut it to that measurement.

*BECAUSE STRETCH LACE IS SOFT, YOU WILL NEED LESS YARDAGE THAN FOR OTHER ELASTIC.*

**SERGER SETTINGS:**

3-thread flatlock stitch

**Stitch length:** Medium

**Stitch width:** Wide

**Needle:** Size 11/75

## How-tos:

1 With right sides together and the straight edges matching, place the flat lace at the slit curve's upper edge. With the lace on top, flat-lock the lace to the lower edge of the slip. Serge slowly, pulling the lace and fabric straight in front of the presser foot around the curves and easing the lace to the slip, especially around the curves. Gently pull the stitching flat.

TEST FIRST. IF THE TRICOT FABRIC BEGINS TO ROLL UNDER THE FLATLOCKING, SERGE-FINISH THE SLIP EDGES FIRST USING A NARROW BALANCED STITCH AND MATCHING THREAD.

2 Quartermark the stretch lace and the upper slip edge. With right sides together and the lace on top, flatlock the straight edge of the lace to the slip, stretching the lace to fit and leaving several inches of thread chain on both ends. Pull the stitching flat and stretch out the elastic to distribute the tricot fabric evenly within the flatlocked stitch. (Fig. 7-9)

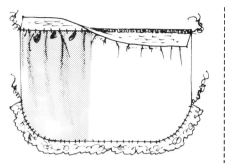

Fig. 7-9 Gather the top of the slip evenly by quartermarking both the stretch lace and the waistline edge before flatlock-seaming them.

ADJUST THE DIFFERENTIAL FEED SLIGHTLY HIGHER THAN THE NORMAL SETTING TO HELP EASE THE TRICOT TO THE LACE WITHOUT STRETCHING OUT THE LACE.

3 Place the slip side edges right sides together, matching the lace edges and the flatlocked seams. Pull the loose thread chains away from the knives on both the upper and under sides and flatlock the side seam, catching the thread chains in the stitching but trimming the ends of the flat lace. (See Fig. 7-3)

4 Knot the thread chains close to the serged stitch on the underside and clip the excess. Dab seam sealant where the stretch lace ends are joined, applying it from the right side on both the upper and lower edges of the waistband.

5 Place one end of the ribbon over the stretch lace seamline, with right sides together and ¼" (6mm) lapped over the lace. Straight-stitch across the ribbon approximately ⅛" (3mm) below the seamline. (Fig. 7-10)

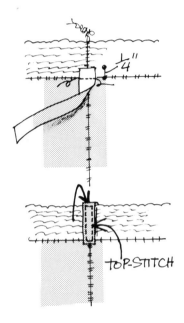

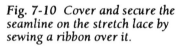

Fig. 7-10 Cover and secure the seamline on the stretch lace by sewing a ribbon over it.

6 Fold the ribbon over the lace seam, around the top of the lace, and down the under-side, slightly past the seam-line. Pin under ¼" and trim any excess. From the right side, top-stitch a rectangle through all thicknesses to secure the ribbon and reinforce the stretch-lace seam.

## FUN FLATLOCK-FINISHED MUFFLER

Decoratively edge a warm muffler with a novel finish. When the flatlock is applied to an edge without letting the stitches hang off the fabric, one side looks like a blanket stitch and the other like balanced serging. (Fig. 7-11)

### SKILLS USED:

Flatlock-finishing; finishing outside corners.

*Fig. 7-11 When using a flatlock stitch for edge-finishing the muffler, you won't pull the stitches flat.*

## Materials needed:

◆ ½ yard (.5m) of 60″-wide (152cm) tightly woven medium- to heavy-weight wool or acrylic fabric

◆ Two spools of buttonhole twist for the needle and upper looper; one spool of all-purpose thread for the lower looper

◆ Seam sealant

### SERGER SETTINGS:

3-thread flatlock stitch

**Stitch length:** Long

**Stitch width:** Wide

**Needle:** Size 14/90

## How-tos:

Test the stitch on scraps of the project fabric. You may need to loosen both the needle-thread and looper-thread tensions to their maximum.

*1* Flatlock-finish the two long edges of the muffler rectangle, wrong side up, leaving a thread chain at both ends. (Fig. 7-12)

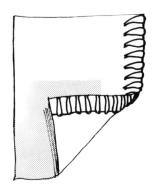

*Fig. 7-12 Finish the edges with the fabric wrong side up so the blanket-like stitching is on the right side.*

*2* Flatlock-finish the two short ends, pulling the thread chains away from the knives on the top of the fabric as you serge over them. Knot all the thread chains close to the stitching, dab seam sealant on the knots, and clip the excess when dry.

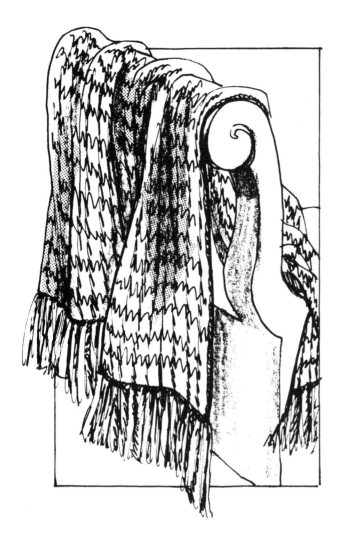

## FLATLOCK-FRINGED THROW

Snuggle up with a warm fringed throw—it's simple to serge and can be made to complement any decor. (Fig. 7-13)

### SKILLS USED:

Flatlock fringing; flatlock-finishing.

## Materials needed:

- 1³/₈ yards (1.3m) of 60"-wide (152cm) loosely woven wool, wool-blend, or acrylic fabric

- Matching serger or all-purpose thread for serging

*Fig. 7-13 Flatlock-fringe the ends and flatlock-finish the long edges.*

### SERGER SETTINGS:

3-thread flatlock stitch

**Stitch length:** Short to medium

**Stitch width:** Medium

**Needle:** Size 11/75

### How-tos:

1 Trim the selvages from the shorter lengthwise-grain edges of the fabric. Mark two flatlocking lines by pulling a thread 3" (7.5cm) from both trimmed edges.

2 Fold the fabric wrong sides together on one pulled-thread line. Leaving a thread chain extending on both ends and allowing the stitches to hang halfway off the edge, flatlock over the fold and pull the stitching flat. Repeat for the opposite edge. (Fig. 7-14)

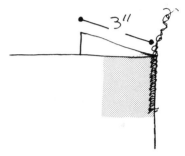

*Fig. 7-14 Fold under the depth you'll be fringing before flatlocking over the fold.*

3 Raise the presser foot and needle and pull the thread chains away from the knife on the underside of the fabric. Insert one long unfinished edge, right side up, under the presser foot with the needle on the outer edge of the first flatlocked line. Lower the presser foot and serge-finish to the outer edge of the flatlocking on the opposite end without letting the stitches hang off the edge. Raise the needle and presser foot, pull the fabric behind the needle, and chain off. (Fig. 7-15)

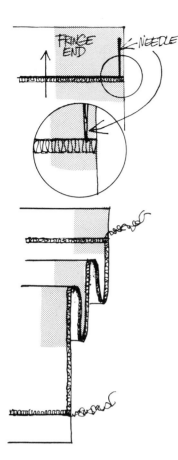

Fig. 7-15 *Begin and end the flatlock-finishing on the outer edges of the previous flatlocking.*

4 Repeat step 3 for the final unfinished edge. Knot the thread chains close to the fabric on each corner and clip the excess.

5 Fringe the throw on the two shorter edges, pulling out the horizontal threads between the cut edges and the flatlocking.

**FOR EASIEST FRINGING, CLIP FROM THE CUT EDGE TO (BUT NOT THROUGH) THE STITCHING EVERY 4" (10CM).**

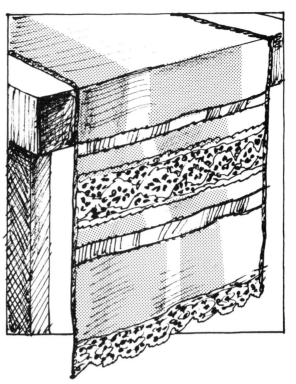

# EMBELLISHED TABLE RUNNER

Give your table a lavish appearance with this Victorian-inspired runner. It looks like an heirloom, but you can make it in no time. (Fig. 7-16)

### SKILLS USED:

Flatlocking to attach lace and ribbon; serge-finished edges.

## Materials needed:

◆ 1/2 yard (.5m) of 60"-wide (152cm) light- to medium-weight woven fabric

◆ 2 yards (1.85m) of ³/₄" -wide (2cm) satin ribbon

◆ One yard (.95m) of 1¹/₂"-wide (4cm) or wider flat lace with straight edges

◆ One yard (.95m) of 1"-wide (2.5cm) or wider flat lace with one scalloped edge, matching or similar to the other lace

◆ Matching serger or all-purpose thread for serging

Fig. 7-16 *Attach lace and ribbon with flatlocking to decorate the runner.*

**IF THE LACE AND RIBBON ARE A DIFFERENT COLOR THAN THE FABRIC, USE THREAD MATCHING THE LACE AND RIBBON WHEN APPLYING THEM AND THREAD MATCHING THE FABRIC FOR SERGE-FINISHING THE EDGES.**

◆ Seam sealant

## Cutting directions:

■ Cut one 54" by 15" (137cm by 38cm) rectangle from the fabric.

■ Cut both pieces of lace into two equal lengths.

■ Cut the ribbon into four equal lengths.

### SERGER SETTINGS:

3-thread flatlock stitch

**Stitch length:** Short

**Stitch width:** Narrow to medium

**Needle:** Size 11/75

## How-tos:

1. Serge-finish both short ends of the rectangle and press ½" (1.3cm) to the wrong side on both ends.

2. Center the wrong side of one piece of scalloped-edge lace on the right side of one pressed allowance, with the straight edge of the lace matching the fold and the lace ends extending past the edge. Flatlock the lace to the runner, then pull the stitching flat, but do not trim the lace or the thread chains. (Fig. 7-17)

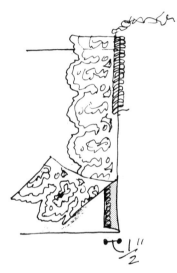

Fig. 7-17 *Flatlock scalloped lace to cover the ends of the runner.*

*SERGE SLOWLY, BEING SURE TO CATCH ALL THE LAYERS IN THE SERGING AND ALLOWING THE STITCHES TO HANG HALFWAY OFF THE EDGE.*

3. Repeat step 2 for the opposite end.

4. Lightly press-mark the runner, wrong sides together, 6" (15cm) from the scalloped-lace edge on both ends. With the lace edge underneath and following instructions in step 2 for the lace application, flatlock one ribbon piece to the runner on the pressed fold. Pull the ribbon and runner flat.

5. Fold the fabric even with the opposite long edge of the ribbon, with the ribbon on top. Flatlock the ribbon to the runner and pull the stitching flat. (Fig. 7-18)

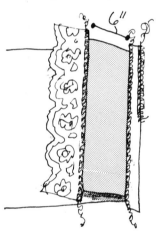

Fig. 7-18 *Fold the fabric even with the ribbon edge to flatlock the second side.*

6. Repeat steps 4 and 5 for the opposite end.

7. Lightly press a line 1" (2.5cm) past the ribbon and flatlock the wider lace to the runner, following the previous instructions.

8. Repeat step 7 for the opposite end.

9. Press a line 1" ( 2.5cm) past the wider lace and flatlock the other ribbon to the runner, following the previous instructions.

10. Repeat step 9 for the opposite end.

11. Serge-finish the long edges from the right side, folding the thread chains to the underside and catching them in the stitching. Dab seam sealant on the thread chain ends and clip the excess close to the serging on the underside. (Fig. 7-19)

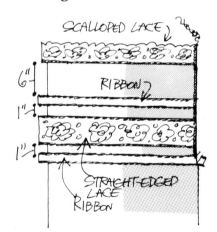

Fig. 7-19 *Trim off the ribbon and lace ends with the knives as you serge-finish the sides.*

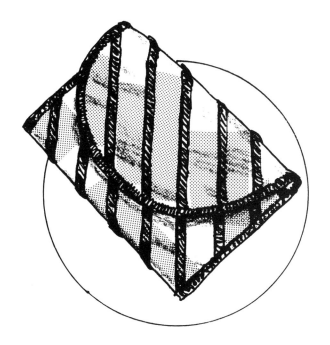

# FAST FLATLOCKED ENVELOPE BAG

When you need an evening bag to coordinate with a special outfit, serge one in a jiffy. No one will believe you didn't pay a fortune for it! (Fig. 7-20)

**SKILLS USED:**

Flatlocking folds; serged seams; serge-finished edges.

## Materials needed:

◆ ⅓ yard (.3m) of woven special-occasion fabric, such as taffeta

◆ ⅓ yard (.3m) of fusible fleece

◆ ⅓ yard (.3m) of heavy fusible interfacing

◆ ⅓ yard (.3m) of paper-backed fusible web

◆ One large snap

◆ Buttonhole twist for the loopers; serger or all-purpose thread for the needle (match the thread color to the fabric for a subtle tone-on-tone look)

◆ Seam sealant

*Fig. 7-20 Serge decorative flatlocking on the fabric before fusing it to fleece and completing the bag.*

## Cutting directions:

■ Cut two 18″ by 12″ (46cm by 30.5cm) rectangles from the fabric.

■ Cut one 18″ by 12″ (46cm by 30.5cm) rectangle each from the fleece, interfacing, and web.

*AFTER SERGE-DECORATING AND ASSEMBLING THE FABRIC LAYERS, YOU WILL TRIM THE FUSED FABRIC TO A SLIGHTLY SMALLER SIZE.*

**SERGER SETTINGS:**

3-thread flatlock stitch for decorative; 3-thread balanced stitch for finishing and seaming

**Stitch length:** Short

**Stitch width:** Medium

**Needle:** Size 11/75

## How-tos:

When fusing the fleece, interfacing, and web, follow the manufacturer's instructions.

1 Fuse the fleece rectangle to the wrong side of one fabric rectangle and the interfacing to the wrong side of the other.

2 Lightly press-mark parallel diagonal lines 1½″ (4cm) apart on the interfaced rectangle, folding the fabric wrong sides together.

3 Adjust your serger for flatlocking and serge over the folds, wrong sides together, pulling the stitching flat after each row.

*BE SURE TO ALLOW THE STITCHES TO HANG HALFWAY OFF THE EDGE BECAUSE IT CAN BE DIFFICULT TO PULL AN INTERFACED FABRIC FLAT AFTER FLATLOCKING.*

4 Fuse the web to the fleece on the other rectangle. Remove the paper backing and fuse the fleece to the back of the interfaced rectangle. (Fig. 7-21)

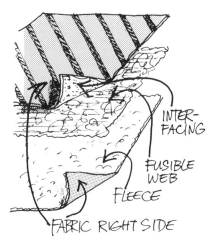

*Fig. 7-21 Sandwich the web between the fabric/interfacing rectangle and the fleece/fabric rectangle and fuse the layers together.*

*YOU MAY NEED TO SMOOTH THE FABRIC AFTER FUSING BY PRESSING FROM THE FABRIC SIDE OF BOTH RECTANGLES.*

5 Cut a 10″ by 16″ (25.5cm by 40.5cm) rectangle from the fused fabric. Using a plate as a guide, round both corners on one short end. Dab seam sealant on the cut ends of the flatlocking and allow them to dry.

6 Adjust your serger to a balanced stitch. With the flatlocked side up, serge-finish the short unrounded end. Fold 5″ (12.5cm) of that end to the wrong side to form the bag. (Fig. 7-22)

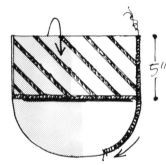

*Fig. 7-22 After folding the straight end to the wrong side, serge around the unfinished edges of the bag.*

7 With the folded portion of the bag up, begin at one corner and serge around the outer edges of the bag, ending at the opposite corner. Knot the thread chains close to the bag, dab seam sealant on the knots, and clip the excess when dry.

8 Fold down the flap and hand-stitch half of the snap to the center of the underside edge. Hand-stitch the other snap section to the bag.

# PINCUSHION IN A TEACUP

Feature your serging skills by flatlocking over narrow ribbon on this charming project. (Fig. 7-23)

## SKILLS USED:

Flatlocking over ribbon; filler-cord gathering; serging curves.

## Materials needed:

◆ ¼ yard (.2m) or a 9″ (23cm) square of tightly woven cotton or cotton-blend fabric

◆ 2½ yards (2.4m) of ⅛″-wide (3mm) ribbon, for testing, flatlocking to the fabric, and a decorative bow

◆ Several yards of filler cord, such as crochet thread or pearl cotton

◆ Polyester fiberfill

◆ Matching serger or all-purpose thread for the needle and lower looper; monofilament nylon thread for the upper looper

◆ Seam sealant

◆ One teacup

## Cutting directions:

Using a plate or lid as a guide, cut a circle approximately 9″ (23cm) in diameter from the fabric.

## SERGER SETTINGS:

3-thread flatlock stitch for flatlocking over ribbon; 3-thread balanced stitch for filler-cord gathering

**Stitch length:** Long for flatlocking; medium for gathering

**Stitch width:** Medium

**Needle:** Size 11/75

*Fig. 7-23 If the teacup has a matching saucer, use it to hold stray buttons or other small notions.*

## How-tos:

1 Place the ribbon under the back and over the front of the presser foot between the needle and the knives, just as you would for serging over filler cord. (See Fig. 4-1)

*FOR ACCURACY IN GUIDING THE RIBBON, THREAD IT THROUGH THE FOOT'S TAPE GUIDE OR AN OPTIONAL BEADING FOOT, IF EITHER IS AVAILABLE.*

2 Hold the ribbon taut in front of and behind the presser foot and serge over it for about 1". Fold the circle in half, wrong sides together.

3 Raise the needle and presser foot and insert the fabric, positioning the fold under the center of the ribbon. (The ribbon and stitches will both hang halfway off the fabric edge when serged.) Flatlock the ribbon to the circle, serging over the ribbon for an additional 1" (2.5cm) past the edge. Raise the needle and presser foot, pull the fabric and ribbon behind the needle, and chain off. Pull the stitches flat. (Fig. 7-24)

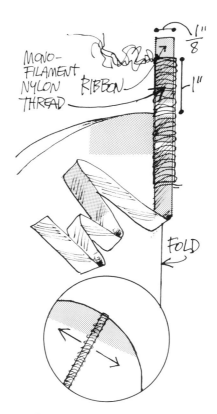

Fig. 7-24 *Let both the ribbon and stitches hang halfway off the fabric when serging, then pull both sides to flatten the stitches.*

*BE CAREFUL NOT TO CUT OR SEW THROUGH THE RIBBON WHILE SERGING OVER IT. BECAUSE OF THE MONOFILAMENT THREAD IN THE UPPER LOOPER, YOU MAY NEED TO LOOSEN THE UPPER LOOPER-THREAD TENSION. REMEMBER TO TEST FIRST.*

4 Refold the circle parallel to and 1" (2.5cm) from the flatlocked ribbon. Flatlock another piece of ribbon, following the instructions in steps 2 and 3. Repeat, flatlocking another ribbon piece 1" (2.5cm) past the opposite side of the center ribbon.

5 Rotate the circle slightly and refold it in half. Flatlock three ribbon pieces to the circle 1" (2.5cm) apart, crossing the other flatlocked ribbons. (Fig. 7-25)

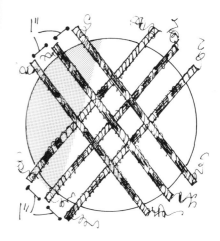

Fig. 7-25 *Cross three rows of flatlocked ribbon over the original three.*

6 Adjust your serger to a balanced stitch. Place two strands of filler cord under the back and over the front of the presser foot, between the needle and knives or use a special beading foot. Slowly serge over them for a few inches, guiding them between the needle and knives without stitching into or cutting them. Fold the ribbon ends to the underside of the circle. With the circle right side up, insert the edge under the presser foot and filler cord and serge around the outer edge. Serge slowly and move the fabric straight in front of the presser foot as you serge over the curved edge, gently pulling the ribbon ends to the underside so they lay flat under the stitching. (Fig. 7-26)

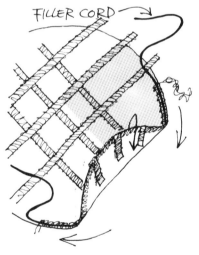

FILLER CORD

Fig. 7-26 Reinforce the ribbon ends by pulling them to the underside and serging over them on both the top and underside as you serge over the filler cord.

7 When you reach the beginning stitches, pull the beginning end of the filler cord to the left of the presser foot and the needle, stopping serging when the needle reaches the beginning stitching. Raise the needle and presser foot, pull the fabric and ending filler cord behind the needle, and chain off. Clip the excess ribbon ends and dab them with seam sealant.

8 Pull the filler cord to gather the circle edges, right side out. Pack the center tightly with fiberfill and pull up the edges completely, knotting the filler cord ends.

9 Place the filled circle in a teacup with the gathered edges down. For permanency, you may choose to glue the fabric to the cup bottom. Tie a decorative bow on the teacup handle with the remaining narrow ribbon.

# EXPANDABLE DESIGNER BELT

Add this fabulous fashion accessory to your wardrobe. You'll find comparable belts in better stores at many times the cost. (Fig. 7-27)

SKILLS USED:

Flatlocking folds; serge-finished edges.

## Materials needed:

- 5" (12.5cm) length of 45"-wide (114cm) *Ultrasuede* or other synthetic suede fabric

- 5" by 24" (12.5cm by 61cm) rectangle of matching lining fabric

- 5" by 27" (12.5cm by 68.5cm) rectangle of heavy fusible interfacing

- 5" by 24" (12.5cm by 61cm) rectangle of fusible fleece

- 5" by 24" (12.5cm by 61cm) rectangle of paper-backed fusible web

- 12" (30.5cm) of 1"-wide (2.5cm) braided elastic for size large or 9" (23cm) for size small

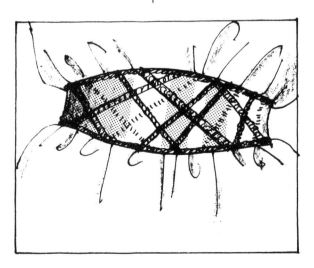

Fig. 7-27 Serge random rows of flatlocking from both sides of the fabric to create a unique design.

- Two pant hook-and-eye sets
- Matching or contrasting serger or all-purpose thread for serging; matching all-purpose thread for the sewing machine
- Seam sealant

## Cutting directions:

- Cut two 8½″ by 3″ (22cm by 7.5cm) rectangles of the *Ultrasuede* for size medium/large or two 6½″ by 3″ (16.5cm by 7.5cm) rectangles for size small/medium for the elastic casings.

THE SMALL/MEDIUM SIZE WILL FIT A 23″ TO 27″ WAIST AND THE MEDIUM/LARGE SIZE WILL FIT A 28″ TO 33″ WAIST.

- Cut two 3″ by 1¾″ (7.5cm by 4.4cm) rectangles of the *Ultrasuede* and the interfacing for the back tabs.

DIVIDE THE INTERFACING INTO TWO PIECES, ONE 3″ BY 5″ (7.5CM BY 12.5CM) AND ONE 24″ BY 5″ (61CM BY 12.5CM). CUT THE BACK TAB RECTANGLES OUT OF THE SMALLER PIECE.

- The belt front will be cut later from the remaining *Ultrasuede*.

SERGER SETTINGS:

3-thread flatlock stitch for the decorative design; 3-thread balanced stitch for finishing

**Stitch length:** Short

**Stitch width:** Narrow

**Needle:** Size 14/90

## How-tos:

1 Adjust your serger for flatlocking. Cut the largest possible rectangle of the remaining *Ultrasuede* and serge a random decorative design on it, featuring both sides of the flatlocked stitching. Fold the piece with wrong sides together to position loops on the right side and fold it opposite to display the ladder stitches. Pull the stitches flat after each row.

FOR MORE TEXTURE, FLATLOCK WITH WRONG SIDES TOGETHER AND A SLIGHTLY TIGHTENED NEEDLE TENSION TO RAISE THE STITCH, ADDING "CORDED FLATLOCKING" TO THE DESIGN. (FIG. 7-28)

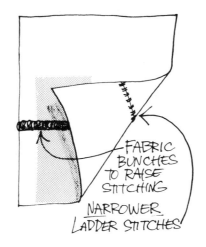

FABRIC BUNCHES TO RAISE STITCHING

NARROWER LADDER STITCHES

*Fig. 7-28 Tighten the needle tension to create corded flatlocking.*

2 With the iron against the fleece side, fuse the fleece to the wrong side of the flatlocked *Ultrasuede* and fuse the interfacing to the wrong side of the lining. Fuse the paper-backed web to the interfacing. Remove the paper backing and, with the lining side up, fuse the *Ultrasuede* and lining wrong sides together.

FOLLOW THE MANUFACTURER'S INSTRUCTIONS FOR ALL FUSING. WHEN FUSING THE *ULTRASUEDE*, PLACE IT ON A HEAVY TERRY TOWEL TO AVOID FLATTENING THE NAP.

3 Using the grid, cut the belt front from the fused fabric. Dab seam sealant on the ends of each flatlocked line and allow it to dry. (Fig. 7-29)

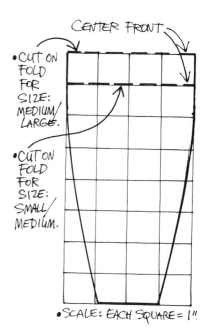

CENTER FRONT

- CUT ON FOLD FOR SIZE: MEDIUM/LARGE.
- CUT ON FOLD FOR SIZE: SMALL/MEDIUM.
- SCALE: EACH SQUARE = 1″.

*Fig. 7-29 Cut out the belt front from the serge-decorated fabric.*

4 Adjust the serger to a balanced stitch. Serge-finish both long edges of the belt and then the short ends. Dab the thread chains with seam sealant and clip them close to the belt when dry.

*FIRST TEST THE SERGE-FINISHING ON SCRAPS OF THE FUSED FABRIC. YOU MAY NEED TO WIDEN THE STITCH SLIGHTLY TO ADJUST FOR THE MULTIPLE LAYERS OF THE BELT FRONT.*

5 Cut the elastic into two equal lengths. To form the elastic casings, fold the two larger rectangles over the elastic, with the fabric wrong sides together. Line up the cut edges of the fabric and elastic on one end, with the elastic against the inside fold. Straight-stitch across the end with a 1/8″ (3mm) seam allowance.

6 Match and straight-stitch the longer cut edges together, with a 1/8″ (3mm) seam allowance. Then line up the opposite short end edges and straight-stitch across them with a 1/8″ (3mm) seam allowance. (Fig. 7-30)

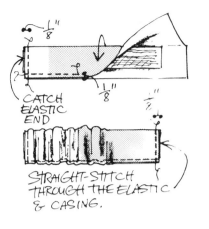

Fig. 7-30 *Straight-stitch one end and the lower edge of the elastic casing before stretching the elastic to meet the opposite end.*

7 Lap one end of the belt front 3/8″ (1cm) over a short end of one encased elastic strip, centering the strip under the belt front with the seam toward the bottom of the belt. Top-stitch along the serge-finishing needleline to join the sections. Repeat for the other end of the belt front. (Fig. 7-31)

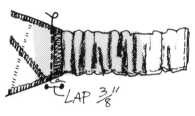

Fig. 7-31 *Lap and top-stitch the elastic casing to the belt ends.*

8 Trim 1/4″ (6mm) from both the length and width of the tab interfacing rectangles. Center and fuse an interfacing rectangle to the wrong side of both *Ultrasuede* tab rectangles.

9 Smooth out both ends of the belt by sliding the casing fullness toward the center. Fold and center a tab around both belt ends, lapping the tab edges 3/8″ (1cm) on both the top and underside. Matching the cut edges, top-stitch with a 1/8″ (3mm) seam allowance. (Fig. 7-32)

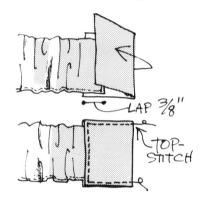

Fig. 7-32 *On both ends of the belt, fold the tab section in half and sandwich the elastic-casing end between the layers.*

10 Hand-stitch the hooks and eyes to the tab sections to secure the belt.

# Notes

# 8 Perfecting Decorative Serging

Using balanced stitching, rolled edges, and flat-locking, you have a variety of attractive serging choices. But when you add decorative threads, your ornamental options are enhanced tremendously.

Any contrasting thread can be decorative when displayed on the right side of a garment or project. You can use lighter-weight thread, such as serger, all-purpose, and even buttonhole twist, with little difficulty. But a variety of special threads are available to expand your decorative options. Woolly nylon, medium-weight rayon thread, pearl cotton, pearl rayon, and crochet thread are all favorites for serging projects.

Serging with most heavier decorative thread is not difficult with a little practice and a few established techniques:

- Use decorative thread in the upper looper when featuring a balanced stitch, rolled edge (see Chapter 6), or flatlocking loops (see Chapter 7). Also use it in the lower looper on a balanced stitch when both sides of the fabric will show. Use it in the needle only to feature flatlocking ladder stitches. (Fig. 8-1)

- On most serger models, use a looper threader or thread cradle to help get decorative thread through the looper eyes more easily. (See Fig. 1-4)

- Always test the stitch on scraps of the project fabric before beginning on the actual project. Test on long strips when possible so that you can make adjustments without raising the presser foot or serging on and off.

REMEMBER TO MAKE ONLY ONE ADJUSTMENT AT A TIME AND CHECK THE RESULTS AS YOU TEST. (SEE PAGE 6) WHEN A THREAD IS HEAVY, STRETCHY, OR HAS MORE TEXTURE, IT WILL PROBABLY NEED LOOSER TENSION. WHEN A THREAD IS FINE OR SLIPPERY, IT WILL PROBABLY NEED TIGHTER TENSION.

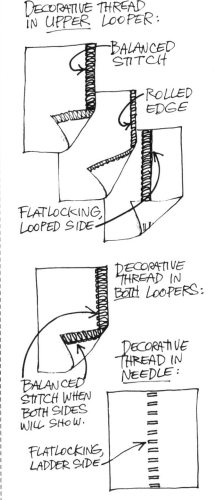

Fig. 8-1 Decide where to use decorative thread, depending on the stitch you want to feature.

- With some heavier threads, such as pearl cotton, you may not be able to loosen the tension enough. In that case, remove the thread from the first thread guide past the telescoping thread stand. If the tension is still too tight, remove the thread from the tension dial or place a piece of transparent tape over the slot, if the tension discs are inset. (Fig. 8-2)

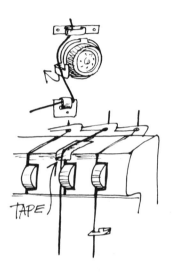

*Fig. 8-2 If you can't loosen the tension enough on heavy decorative thread, remove it from the tension mechanism.*

- Be sure your decorative thread is flowing freely and doesn't become caught on the spool, under the spool, or somewhere on the machine. If the thread is in a ball or skein, rewind it onto a spool or cone for the easiest serging or reel off enough at a time so that the thread feeds freely into the machine without pulling or tangling.

- Experiment with the stitch length and width for the most attractive option. Remember that you will often need to readjust the tension when you change the stitch.

- A satin-length stitch is often used for decorative serging because it simulates binding or piping. To perfect a satin stitch, shorten the length until the thread completely covers the fabric underneath it. A finer thread will need a shorter stitch than a heavier thread. Remember to tighten the tension to compensate for the shorter stitch. (See page 8)

WHEN ADJUSTING FOR A SATIN STITCH USING HEAVIER THREAD, BEGIN TESTING AT A MEDIUM LENGTH AND SHORTEN THE STITCH TO PERFECT IT. IF YOU BEGIN WITH THE LENGTH TOO SHORT, THE THREAD CAN JAM UNDER THE PRESSER FOOT.

- When using decorative thread, always serge slowly for the best results.

FOR MORE DETAILS ON DECORATIVE SERGING, REFER TO CHAPTER 12 IN *ABCS OF SERGING*. DECORATIVE OPTIONS ARE ALSO FEATURED IN *SERGED GARMENTS IN MINUTES* INCLUDING DECORATIVE CLOSURES IN CHAPTER 8, SPECIAL POCKET TREATMENTS IN CHAPTER 9, AND NOVELTY BOWS AND ROSETTES IN CHAPTER 11.

# RUFFLE-TRIMMED V-NECK TOP

Lettuce the edge of a fabric strip to quickly decorate a simple pullover top. (Fig. 8-3)

SKILLS USED:

Serged seams; lettuced rolled edges; flatlock gathering; serged, turned, and top-stitched hems.

## *Materials needed:*

◆ Basic pullover top pattern designed for knits with a faced V neckline, long hemmed sleeves, and a hemmed lower edge

SELECT THE PATTERN SIZE BY COMPARING YOUR BUST MEASUREMENT TO THOSE ON THE BACK OF THE PATTERN ENVELOPE.

◆ Cotton or cotton-blend interlock fabric, following the pattern yardage requirements plus an additional ⅙ yard (.2m) for the ruffle

◆ Fusible knit interfacing, following the pattern yardage requirements

◆ Matching or contrasting serger or all-purpose thread for lettucing; matching serger or all-purpose thread for all other serging; matching all-purpose thread for the sewing machine

◆ Six ⅜" (1cm) buttons

◆ Seam sealant

- Cut one front, one back, two sleeves, one back facing, and one front facing from the interlock.

*TRANSFER THE PATTERN MARKINGS TO THE WRONG SIDE OF THE FABRIC, ESPECIALLY WHEN USING A PATTERN WITH 1/4" (6MM) SEAM ALLOWANCES.*

- Cut one front and one back facing from the interfacing.

- Cut two 60" by 2" (152cm by 5cm) strips of interlock, with the greatest stretch going the length of the strips.

### SERGER SETTINGS:

3- or 3/4-thread balanced stitch for seaming and finishing; 3-thread rolled-edge stitch for lettucing; 3-thread flatlock stitch for gathering

**Stitch length:** Medium for seaming and finishing; short for lettucing; long for gathering

**Stitch width:** Wide for seaming and finishing; narrow for lettucing; medium for gathering

**Needle:** Size 11/75

### How-tos:

When serge-seaming 1/4" (6mm) allowances, just skim the fabric edge with the knives. When the allowances are 5/8" (1.5cm), serge-seam with the needle (the left needle of a 3/4-thread stitch) on the seamline and trim approximately 3/8" (1cm) with the knives.

## Cutting directions:

- Compare your bust, waist, hip, and back waist-length measurements to those on the pattern envelope and make any necessary pattern alterations.

*Fig. 8-3  On this top, you'll gather the ruffle with flatlocking to avoid the bulk of the serged seam allowances on other gathering techniques.*

*CHECK THE SLEEVE LENGTH BY PINNING THE FRONT, BACK, AND SLEEVE PATTERN PIECES TOGETHER AND HOLDING THEM OVER YOUR SHOULDER. BEND YOUR ARM SLIGHTLY FOR THE MOST ACCURATE MEASUREMENT, AND REMEMBER TO ALLOW FOR THE HEM ALLOWANCE.*

*TEST SERGE ON SCRAPS OF THE PROJECT FABRIC, BOTH ON THE LENGTHWISE AND CROSSWISE GRAINLINES. ALSO TEST SEAMING TWO LAYERS. IF THE SEAM STRETCHES WHEN SERGED, LENGTHEN THE STITCH SLIGHTLY, ADJUST TO A HIGHER DIFFERENTIAL-FEED SETTING, OR EASE-PLUS MANUALLY. (SEE FIG. 1-17) IF THE SEAM PUCKERS, ADJUST THE DIFFERENTIAL FEED TO ITS LOWEST SETTING AND SEW USING TAUT SERGING. (SEE FIG. 1-18)*

1 Adjust your serger to a rolled-edge stitch. With right sides together, serge-seam two short ends of the narrow strips to form one long strip.

2 Adjust the differential feed to its lowest setting for the lettucing. From the right side of the strip, anchor a few stitches into the interlock. Then hold the thread chain behind the presser foot and the interlock edge in the front. Serge the edge, trimming approximately ¼″ (6mm). Repeat for the opposite long edge. (Fig. 8-4)

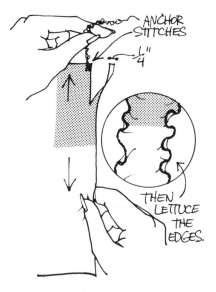

Fig. 8-4 *Hold the strip taut when lettucing with differential feed. Stretch it slightly if you're not using differential feed.*

*IF YOUR SERGER MODEL DOES NOT HAVE DIFFERENTIAL FEED, LETTUCE THE EDGE BY STRETCHING IT SLIGHTLY AS YOU SERGE OVER IT.*

3 Adjust your serger to a 3-thread flatlock stitch and the differential feed to its highest setting (or ease-plus as you serge). Fold the strip, right sides together, and flatlock over the fold, allowing the stitches to hang halfway off the fabric and leaving several inches of thread chain on both ends. Pull the stitching flat. If you want more gathering on the strip, pull out the thread chain on both ends and find the shortest thread, which is the lower looper thread. Gently pull it to add gathering. (Fig. 8-5)

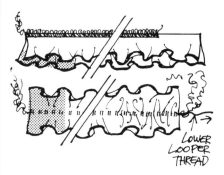

Fig. 8-5 *Flatlock-gather the center of the ruffle. For more gathering, pull the shortest thread on both ends.*

*THE FLATLOCK STITCH CAN BE USED FOR GATHERING JUST AS YOU WOULD A BALANCED STITCH, BUT THE FABRIC CAN BE PULLED FLAT UNDER THE STITCHING. USE FLATLOCK GATHERING WHENEVER YOU WANT TO AVOID A BULKY SEAM ON THE GATHERING LINE.*

4 Adjust the serger to a balanced stitch for serge-seaming and serge-finishing. If necessary, adjust the differential feed to a higher setting to prevent stretching the fabric. With right sides together, serge-seam the shoulders. Press the seam allowances toward the back.

*SERGE CONTINUOUSLY FROM ONE SEAM TO THE OTHER, LEAVING SEVERAL INCHES OF THREAD CHAIN BETWEEN. AFTER SEAMING, CLIP APART THE CENTER OF THE THREAD CHAIN.*

5 Following the manufacturer's instructions, fuse the interfacing to the wrong side of the facings.

6 Straight-stitch the front and back facings, right sides together, and press the seam allowances open. Beginning from the right side of the fabric at the lower edge of the front facing, serge-finish the outer edges, just skimming the fabric with the knives. Knot the thread-chain ends close to the fabric and clip the excess.

7 Place the facing and bodice right sides together, matching the pattern markings. Straight-stitch, pivoting at the center-front V. Clip to the point of the V, being careful not to cut through the stitching, and trim the seam allowances.

**8** Carefully press the facing and seam allowances away from the garment. From the right side, under-stitch through the seam allowances ¹/₈″ (3mm) from the seamline.

**9** Press the facing to the wrong side. From the right side, stitch-in-the-ditch of the shoulder seams to secure the facing.

**10** Lightly press-mark the center front, folding it in half with wrong sides together. Pin the ruffle, with the ladder stitches up, to the right side of the top, matching the ruffle seam to the center back and running both ends around the neckline and down the center front to the lower edge, ¹/₄″ (6mm) from the neckline and the center-front marking. Top-stitch down the center of the ruffle over the flatlocking using a long, narrow zigzag. Trim the ruffle ends even with the lower front edge. (Fig. 8-6)

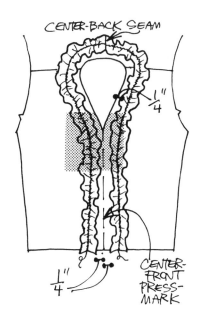

*Fig. 8-6 Use a narrow zigzag to top-stitch the ruffle around the neckline and down the front.*

**11** Serge-seam the sleeves to the top, right sides together, matching the markings and with the garment on top.

**12** Serge-finish both lower sleeve edges and press the hem allowances to the wrong side.

**13** Serge-seam one side/sleeve seam, right sides together, matching the underarm seamlines and folding out the sleeve hem allowance. Press the seam allowances toward the back.

**14** Serge-finish the lower edge of the top, catching the ends of the ruffle in the serging.

**15** Serge the other side/sleeve seam, following the instructions in step 13, then press up the lower hem allowance.

**16** On all the hems, tuck the thread chains inside the hem allowance. Top-stitch the hems in place from the right side, using a long stitch and stretching slightly as you sew. On the lower-edge hem, begin and end under the ruffle edges without stitching over them. (Fig. 8-7)

*Fig. 8-7 Top-stitch through the garment and hem allowance but not through the ruffle.*

**17** Evenly space and sew on buttons, beginning at the center front ¹/₂″(1.3cm) below the V and ending 4″ (10cm) above the lower hemline.

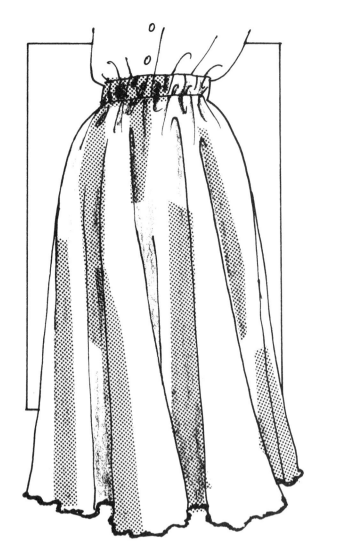

## LETTUCE-EDGED CIRCLE SKIRT

Coordinate this attractive skirt with the previous ruffle-trimmed top for a fashionable ensemble. (Fig. 8-8)

**SKILLS USED:**

Serged seams; serged pull-on waistband; lettuced rolled edges.

*Fig. 8-8 Two seams, an easy-to-serge waistband, and a lettuced rolled edge are all you'll need to make this circle skirt.*

## Materials needed:

◆ Circle or half-circle skirt pattern with a cut-on elastic waistband casing

◆ Soft lightweight cotton or cotton-blend interlock, following the pattern yard-age requirements

◆ Sew-through waistline elastic, the length specified on the pattern in a width you prefer

◆ Matching or contrasting serger or all-purpose thread for lettucing; matching serger or all-purpose thread for all other serging; matching all-purpose thread for the sewing machine

## Cutting directions:

■ If the elastic width is different than specified in the pattern requirements, adjust both the front and back pattern pieces for a waistline casing double the elastic width plus ½" (1.3cm). Extend the casing ends straight up from the side edges of the waistline.

**CHECK TO BE SURE THE TOTAL SKIRT WAISTLINE MEASUREMENT IS LARGE ENOUGH TO PULL OVER YOUR HIPS.**

■ Cut one skirt front and one skirt back.

**SERGER SETTINGS:**

3-thread balanced stitch for seaming; 3-thread rolled-edge stitch for lettucing

**Stitch length:** Medium for seaming sides; long for seaming elastic; short for lettucing

**Stitch width:** Wide for seaming; narrow for lettucing

**Needle:** Size 11/75

## How-tos:

When using a pattern with ⁵/₈″ (1.5cm) seam allowances, serge-seam with the needle on the seamline and trim approximately ³/₈″ (1cm) with the knives.

*TEST SEAMING ON SCRAPS OF THE PROJECT FABRIC. IF THE SEAM STRETCHES WHEN SERGED, LENGTHEN THE STITCH SLIGHTLY, ADJUST TO A HIGHER DIFFERENTIAL-FEED SETTING, OR EASE-PLUS MANUALLY. (SEE FIG. 1-17) IF THE SEAM PUCKERS, ADJUST THE DIFFERENTIAL FEED TO ITS LOWEST SETTING AND SEW USING TAUT SERGING. (SEE FIG. 1-18)*

1 With right sides together and beginning at the waist edge, serge-seam the front and back together at both side seams.

*TO HOLD THE LONG EDGES IN PLACE FOR SERGING, PIN PARALLEL TO THE SEAMLINE ABOUT 1/2″ (1.3CM) LEFT OF IT. BE CAREFUL TO REMOVE THE PINS BEFORE THEY REACH THE PRESSER FOOT. OR USE FINGER-PINNING, SECURING ONE END OF THE SEAMLINE WITH THE NEEDLE AND PRESSER FOOT AND HOLDING THE MATCHED EDGES AT THE SEAMLINE MIDPOINT AND THE LOWER EDGE. RELEASE THE FABRIC WHEN THE FOOT REACHES YOUR FINGERS. (SEE FIG. 5-7)*

2 Measure the elastic comfortably around your waist and add ¹/₂″ (1.3cm) for lapping. Sew the elastic into a circle by overlapping the ends and zigzagging them together.

3 Using pins, quartermark both the elastic and the waistline edge. Readjust your serger to a long stitch. With the elastic on top and matching the quartermarks, serge-seam the elastic to the wrong side of the waistline edge, stretching the elastic to fit the opening. Lap the serging about ¹/₂″ (1.3cm) before serging off the edge.

*ADJUST THE DIFFERENTIAL FEED TO THE HIGHEST SETTING TO HELP EASE THE FABRIC TO THE ELASTIC AND PREVENT THE ELASTIC FROM STRETCHING OUT.*

4 Using a long straight-stitch, top-stitch the unattached edge of the elastic to the skirt, stretching the elastic as you sew over it. (Fig. 8-9)

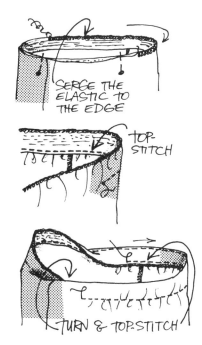

**Fig. 8-9** *Stretch firmly while top-stitching through the elastic.*

*THIS STITCHING WILL HOLD THE ELASTIC FIRMLY IN PLACE WHILE TURNING AND DURING WEARING.*

5 Turn the elastic to the wrong side and enclose it. From the wrong side of the skirt, top-stitch along the serged edge, catching all layers. Use a long stitch and stretch as you sew. Steam the elastic well from the wrong side, being careful not to touch the fabric with the iron.

6 Hang the skirt for 24 hours to allow for any stretching of the fabric. Try on the skirt, mark the hem, and trim on the marked line.

7 Adjust your serger for rolled-edge lettucing and the differential feed to its lowest setting. Beginning close to one side seam with the right side up, anchor a few stitches into the edge of the skirt. To start, hold the thread chain behind the presser foot and the skirt edge in the front. Serge around the skirt bottom, just skimming the edge with the knives. If you're not using differential feed, stretch slightly to ruffle the edge. (See Fig. 8-4) Serge slowly over the seams and lap the stitching ends for about ¹/₂″ (1.3cm), being careful not to cut the beginning stitching. Raise the presser foot and needle, pull the fabric behind the needle, and chain off. Trim the excess thread chain.

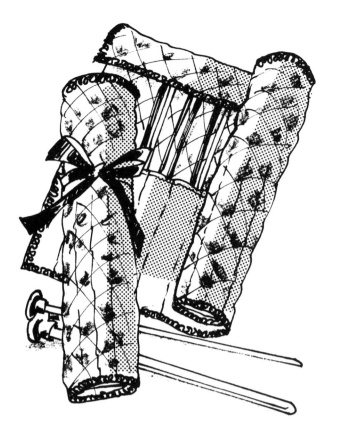

# ROLL-UP KNITTING-NEEDLE CASE

Keep all of your knitting needles and accessories organized and handy in this simple, decoratively serged case. (Fig. 8-10)

### SKILLS USED:

Serge-finished edges using heavy decorative thread.

## Materials needed:

◆ ½ yard (.5m) of 45″-wide (114cm) double-faced quilted fabric

◆ ¼ yard (.25m) of matching or coordinating woven fabric, such as muslin, for the pocket

◆ ¾ yard (.7m) of ⅜″-wide (1cm) ribbon

*Fig. 8-10 Stretch firmly while top-stitching through the elastic.*

◆ Two spools of complementary-color heavy decorative thread such as pearl cotton for the loopers; matching serger or all-purpose thread for the needle; matching all-purpose thread for the sewing machine

◆ Seam sealant

## Cutting directions:

■ Cut one 21″ by 18″ (53.5cm by 46cm) rectangle from the quilted fabric for the case.

■ Cut one 21″ by 8″ (53.5cm by 20.5cm) rectangle from the woven fabric for the pocket.

SERGER SETTINGS:

3-thread balanced stitch

**Stitch length:** Short

**Stitch width:** Wide

**Needle:** Size 14/90

## How-tos:

1 On one long edge of the pocket rectangle, press ¼″ (6mm) to the wrong side and top-stitch. Press an additional ¼″ (6mm) to the wrong side and top-stitch next to the inner fold to secure the hem.

2 Place the unfinished long edge of the pocket rectangle, wrong sides together, on top of one long edge of the quilted fabric, matching the cut edges. Straight-stitch parallel vertical lines, as illustrated, to form pockets for knitting needles and accessories, back-stitching at the upper pocket edge. (Fig. 8-11)

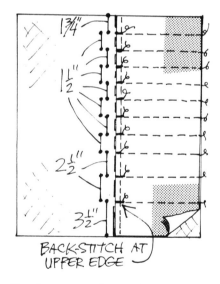

*Fig. 8-11 Straight-stitch to form pockets of various sizes.*

3 Fold the ribbon in half crosswise and pin it to the outside of the case, 8" (20.5cm) down from the upper edge, matching the fold to the cut edge of the case. Machine-baste near the edge to hold it in position. (Fig. 8-12)

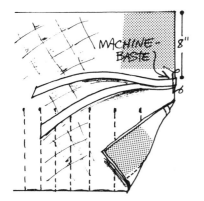

*Fig. 8-12 Align the ribbon fold with the cut edge so that it will be caught in the serge-finishing.*

4 Thread the pearl cotton in both loopers and serger or all-purpose thread in the needle. Loosen the looper-thread tensions almost completely. Adjust for a medium-length, balanced stitch, serging slowly as you test. Gradually shorten the stitch to a satin length, with both the upper and lower looper threads flat and overlocking right on the edge. If the fabric stretches, lengthen the stitch slightly.

IF THE TENSION IS TOO TIGHT, EVEN AFTER LOOSENING THE CONTROLS AS MUCH AS POSSIBLE, FIRST BE SURE THE THREAD HAS NOT BECOME HUNG UP ON ANY OF THE TENSION GUIDES OR THE THREAD STAND. THEN REMOVE IT FROM THE FIRST THREAD GUIDE TO DECREASE THE PRESSURE ON IT. IF THE TENSION IS STILL TOO TIGHT, REMOVE THE THREAD FROM THE TENSION DIAL OR PLACE TRANSPARENT TAPE OVER THE SLOT. (SEE FIG. 8-2)

5 From the right side of the case, serge-finish both the lengthwise edges, catching the ribbon fold in the stitching. Serge on and off at the corners, holding the thread chain taut as you begin. Then serge-finish both crosswise edges to match. Dab seam sealant on the thread chain at each corner and clip the excess thread when dry.

6 After placing the needles and accessories into the pockets, fold down the top edge over them, roll up the case, and tie it closed with the ribbon.

# EASY-TO-WEAR SCARF HOLDER

Wear a scarf in style without tricky knots or folds—just pull the ends through this serge-decorated tube! (Fig. 8-13)

### SKILLS USED:

Corded flatlock using rayon thread; serged seams; rolled-edge finishing.

*Fig. 8-13 Keep any scarf neatly in place with a tubular scarf holder.*

## Materials needed:

- ⅛ yard (.1m) of quilted metallic lamé fabric
- One spool of contrasting (or coordinating) medium-weight rayon thread, such as *Decor 6* or *Designer 6*, for the upper looper; matching serger or all-purpose thread for the needle and lower looper

*IF THE RAYON THREAD FALLS OFF THE SPOOL WHILE YOU'RE SERGING WITH IT, YOU'LL ALSO NEED A THREAD NET TO KEEP IT NEATLY IN PLACE. (FIG. 8-14)*

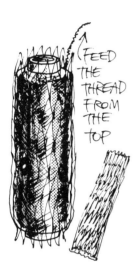

Fig. 8-14 Use a thread net to keep slippery thread from falling off the spool and tangling.

- Seam sealant

### SERGER SETTINGS:

3-thread flatlock stitch for decorative; 3-thread balanced stitch for seaming; 3-thread rolled-edge stitch for finishing

**Stitch length:** Short for flatlocking and rolled edge; medium for seaming

**Stitch width:** Narrow

**Needle:** Size 11/75

## How-tos:

1 Thread your serger with rayon thread in the upper looper and serger or all-purpose thread in the needle and lower looper. Adjust for flatlocking by loosening the needle tension and tightening the lower looper tension. (See Fig. 7-1) Test and perfect the stitch on a fold of the quilted fabric, with wrong sides together. Then tighten the needle tension slightly to raise the stitch for corded flatlocking. (See Fig. 7-28)

2 Fold the fabric, wrong sides together, on a prequilted line. Leaving a thread chain at the ends, flatlock over the fold with the stitches hanging halfway off the fabric. Do not clip the thread chains. Pull the stitching as flat as possible (it won't be completely flat because of the raised cording).

3 Repeat the flatlocking on five parallel quilted lines.

4 Repeat the flatlocking on lines midway between each of the original flatlocked lines.

5 Cut out two scarf ring sections, following the pattern grid. (Fig. 8-15)

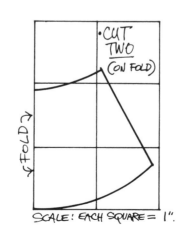

Fig. 8-15 Cut out the scarf ring after serging the corded flatlocking.

*TO MAKE SURE THE FLATLOCKED ROWS WILL MATCH AT THE TOP AND BOTTOM EDGES OF THE TUBE, CUT OUT ONE SECTION FIRST. THEN PLACE IT, RIGHT SIDES TOGETHER, ON THE REMAINING FABRIC AND ALIGN THE DECORATIVE STITCHING ACCURATELY BEFORE CUTTING THE SECOND SECTION.*

6 Adjust your serger to a narrow, balanced stitch. Test on two layers of fabric scraps. Serge-seam the longest edge of the tube, right sides together.

7 Adjust for a rolled-edge stitch by tightening the lower looper and loosening the upper looper slightly and test the stitch. From the right side of the fabric, serge-finish both side edges, stitching slowly to cross the decorative serging neatly.

8 Adjust back to a narrow, balanced stitch and, with right sides together, serge-seam the upper edge. Dab seam sealant on the thread chains and clip the ends close to the fabric when dry.

9 Turn the tube right side out. To wear, thread opposite corners of a scarf through opposite ends of the tube and pull them to tighten the scarf around your neck.

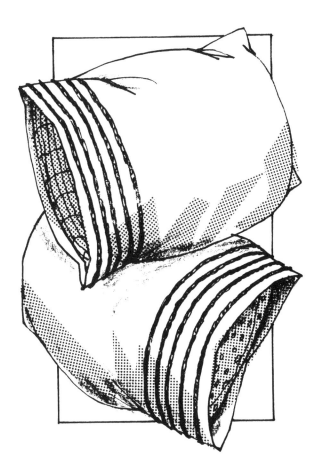

Fig. 8-16 Dress up any bed with heirloom-inspired pintucks.

# DISTINCTIVE PINTUCKED PILLOWCASE

Serge delicate decorative pintucks on a length of fabric, then quickly sew it into a pretty but practical pillowcase. (Fig. 8-16)

### SKILLS USED:

Serged pintucks; serged seams; serged, turned, and top-stitched hem.

## Materials needed:

- One yard (.95m) of tightly woven cotton or cotton-blend fabric

- One spool of matching or coordinating woolly nylon thread for the upper looper; matching serger or all-purpose thread for the needle and lower looper; matching all-purpose thread for the sewing machine

- Air-erasable marker

### SERGER SETTINGS:

3-thread balanced stitch

**Stitch length:** Short for pintucking; medium for seaming and finishing

**Stitch width:** Narrow for pintucking; wide for seaming and finishing

**Needle:** Size 11/75

## How-tos:

Serge-seam using ¼" (6mm) allowances, just skimming the edges with the knives.

1 Fold and press-mark a hem-line, with the fabric wrong sides together, 4" (10cm) from one long edge. Use the marker to draw five parallel lines ⅝" (1.5cm) apart on the right side of the fabric, beginning ¾" (2cm) in from the press-mark. (Fig. 8-17)

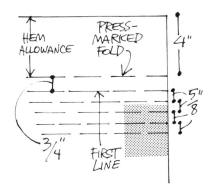

Fig. 8-17 Mark the serging lines after press-marking the hem allowance.

2 Thread your serger with woolly nylon in the upper looper and with serger or all-purpose thread in the needle and lower looper. Adjust to a short, narrow, balanced stitch for pintucking.

*TEST THE STITCH. YOU MAY NEED TO LOOSEN THE UPPER LOOPER TENSION AND TIGHTEN THE LOWER LOOPER TENSION MORE THAN NORMAL TO KEEP THE WOOLLY NYLON FROM STRETCHING AND TIGHTENING THE LOOPS ON THE TOP OF THE STITCH.*

3 Fold the fabric, wrong sides together, on the marked tuck line that is farthest from the press-marking and serge the fold, being careful not to cut the fabric.

4 Continue folding and serging each tuck, stitching them all in the same direction. For accurate parallel spacing, use the width of the presser foot to guide each new row. (Fig. 8-18)

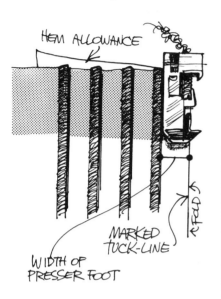

*Fig. 8-18 Use the width of the presser foot as a guide for accurate spacing.*

5 Press the tucks to one side so the top of the serged stitch is up.

**BE CAREFUL WHEN PRESSING BECAUSE A HOT IRON WILL MELT THE NYLON THREAD.**

6 Cut a 41" by 34" (104cm by 86.5cm) rectangle from the pintucked fabric, without cutting any off the long edge nearest the pintucks (to leave the press-marked hem edge intact).

7 Adjust your serger to a wide, medium-length stitch for serge-finishing and serge-seaming. Serge-finish the long edge nearest the pintucking.

8 Fold the rectangle in half crosswise, with right sides together. Match and serge-seam the remaining raw edges. Knot the thread chains and clip the excess. (Fig. 8-19)

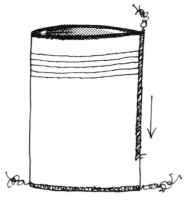

*Fig. 8-19 Serge-seam the side and end of the pillowcase.*

9 Fold the 4" (10cm) hem allowance to the wrong side and top-stitch it in place.

# DECORATIVE WHISK BROOM COVER

Quickly serge decorative braid for this unique project or whenever you want a color-coordinated trim. (Fig. 8-20)

**SKILLS USED:**

Decorative serged braid; serged seams; serged, turned, and top-stitched hem.

*Fig. 8-20 You'll want to keep your whisk broom in plain sight after you add an attractive serged cover.*

## Materials needed:

◆ ¼ yard (.25m) of tightly woven medium-weight fabric

◆ One ball of cotton or acrylic crochet thread and two matching spools or cones of all-purpose thread for the braid

◆ Three spools or cones of serger or all-purpose thread, matching the fabric, for serging; all-purpose thread, matching the fabric, for the sewing machine

◆ 28" (71cm) of ⅝-wide (1.5cm) satin ribbon

◆ Seam sealant

◆ Craft glue

◆ One whisk broom

## Cutting directions:

■ Make a pattern by tracing around the top of the whisk broom to ¾" (2cm) past the broom's stitching line and adding ¼"(6mm) seam allowances. Trim out a curved area for the handle. (Fig. 8-21)

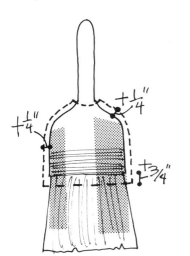

Fig. 8-21 *Trace around the upper edge of the broom, curving out an opening for the handle.*

■ Using the pattern, cut two cover pieces.

■ Cut one 1"-wide (2.5cm) strip three times the width of the broom.

### SERGER SETTINGS:

3-thread balanced stitch

**Stitch length:** Short for decorative; medium for finishing and seaming

**Stitch width:** Wide for decorative and seaming; medium for finishing

**Needle:** Size 11/75

## How-tos:

Serge-seam using ¼" (6mm) allowances, just skimming the edges with the knives.

1 To make the decorative braid, thread your serger with crochet thread in the upper looper and the matching serger or all-purpose thread in the needle and lower looper. Begin testing the decorative stitch at a medium length with a loosened upper looper-thread tension. Turn the handwheel to be sure a thread chain is forming. Shorten the stitch gradually to perfect a satin stitch, with the upper looper thread pulled completely to the edge of the fabric.

2 Serge-finish one long edge of the fabric strip, trimming only a small amount with the knives.

3 Reverse the strip and serge-finish the opposite edge, with the needlelines right next to each other and the decorative thread meeting in the center. (Fig. 8-22)

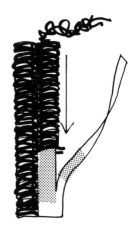

Fig. 8-22 *Make serged braid by serge-finishing both long edges of a fabric strip, with the stitches meeting in the middle.*

*IF YOU HAVEN'T ALREADY MARKED THE NEEDLELINE ON TOP OF THE PRESSER FOOT TO HELP GUIDE YOUR STITCHING ACCURATELY (SEE FIG. 1-9), DO SO BEFORE BEGINNING THE SERGED BRAID.*

4 Change the upper looper to the serger or all-purpose thread that matches the fabric and adjust to a medium-length, medium-width stitch. Place the covers right sides together and serge-seam one side.

5 Serge-finish the curved upper edge. Turn the edge to the wrong side on the serging needleline and top-stitch the upper hem in place.

**6** Lap the wrong side of the serged braid ½" (1.3cm) over the wrong side of the lower edge and top-stitch the braid to the cover. Fold the braid to the right side and top-stitch it into position. (Fig. 8-23)

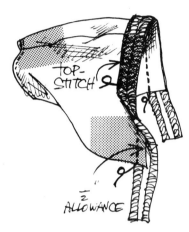

*Fig. 8-23 After lapping and top-stitching the braid to the wrong side, fold the braid to the right side and top-stitch the other edge.*

**7** Matching the braid at the bottom and the curved edge at the top, with right sides together serge-seam the other side. Dab seam sealant on the thread chains and trim the excess when dry.

**8** Slip the cover over the whisk broom and glue the underside of the bottom edge to the broom. Tie the ribbon into a bow around the bottom of the handle and trim the ends diagonally.

# FITTED CARD TABLE COVER

Whether you use your card table for games, extra dining space, or a temporary work surface, you'll love this useful cover. It fits a 34"- or 35"-square table snugly with the aid of *Velcro* closures, and it's washable, too. (Fig. 8-24)

## SKILLS USED:

Serged seams; serge-finishing a fold; serged binding application; serging curves.

## Materials used:

- ◆ 1¼ yards (1.15m) of 45"-wide (114cm) double-faced quilted or synthetic suede fabric

- ◆ Six yards (5.5m) of single-fold matching or contrasting bias tape

- ◆ 12" (30.5cm) of 1½"-wide (4cm) *Velcro*

- ◆ One spool of buttonhole twist and two matching spools or cones of all-purpose thread for decorating the binding

- ◆ Three spools or cones of serger or all-purpose thread, matching the fabric, for serge-seaming; all-purpose thread, matching the fabric, for the sewing machine

- ◆ Seam sealant

## Cutting directions:

- ■ Cut one 40½" by 35" (103cm by 89cm) fabric rectangle.

- ■ Cut two 40½" by 3¼" (103cm by 8cm) fabric rectangles.

## SERGER SETTINGS:

3-thread balanced stitch

**Stitch length:** Short for finishing the binding; medium for seaming

**Stitch width:** Medium for finishing the binding; wide for seaming

**Needle:** Size 14/90

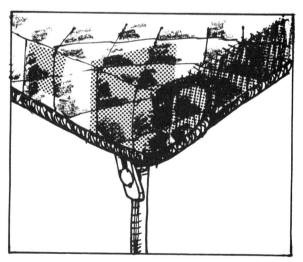

*Fig. 8-24 Cover your card table in style with a fitted, decoratively serged cloth.*

## How-tos:

Serge-seam using ¼" (6mm) allowances, just skimming the fabric edge with the knives.

1. Trim away the ¼" (6mm) seam allowances for 3" (7.5cm) on both ends of the larger rectangle's long edges and on only one long edge of the two smaller rectangles. (Fig. 8-25)

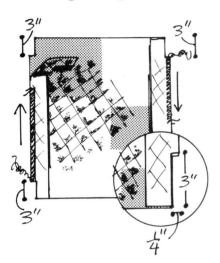

Fig. 8-25 Trim away the seam allowances where the edges will be bound.

2. Matching the edges cut in step 1, serge-seam a narrow rectangle, right sides together, to both long edges of the larger rectangle.

3. Adjust your serger to a short, medium-width stitch. Thread buttonhole twist in the upper looper and matching serger or all-purpose thread in the needle and lower looper. Serge-finish one folded edge of the bias tape from the top side.

TEST FIRST. YOU MAY NEED TO LOOSEN THE UPPER LOOPER TENSION SLIGHTLY SO THAT THE HEAVIER DECORATIVE THREAD INTERLOCKS EXACTLY ON THE EDGE. BEGIN TESTING WITH A MEDIUM-LENGTH STITCH AND ADJUST GRADUALLY TO A SHORTER SATIN LENGTH TO AVOID JAMMING WHEN STARTING.

4. Round all the corners. Fold under ½" (1.3cm) on one end of the binding and position it wrong side up against the wrong side of the fabric with the folded end even with the end of one seam. Before cutting the binding, steam-press to mold it around the curved edges to the end of the next seam, folding the finishing end under ½" (1.3cm). Straight-stitch the binding to the cover along the unserged fold. (Fig. 8-26)

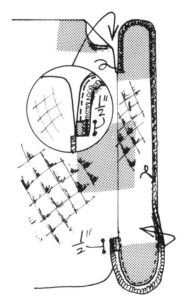

Fig. 8-26 Shape the binding around the curves, straight-stitch it to the wrong side, then wrap and top-stitch it to the right side.

5. Wrap the binding to the right side and top-stitch it in place close to the unattached edge.

6. Repeat steps 4 and 5 for the other three unfinished edges of the cover.

7. Cut the *Velcro* into four 3"-long (7.5cm) pieces and round the corners. Place the hooked sides on the wrong side of the four extending tab sections and top-stitch them into position.

8. Fold the tabs to the right side of the larger rectangle, forming box corners. Mark the placement for the looped sides of the *Velcro* and top-stitch them into position. (Fig. 8-27)

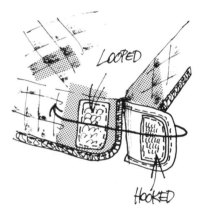

Fig. 8-27 Mark and top-stitch the looped side of the Velcro to align with the hooked side, after forming the box corners.

9. Place the cover on the table and secure it by fastening the *Velcro* at the corners.

# PRETTY PATCHWORK BAG

Decoratively piece scraps of luxury fabric to create a stylish designer bag. (Fig. 8-28)

### SKILLS USED:

Decorative serged piecing; decorative serge-finished edge.

## Materials needed:

- Scraps of *Ultrasuede* or other synthetic suede fabric including two ³/₄" by 45" (2cm by 114cm) strips, or a ¹/₃ yard (.3m) length, for the bag ties

- ¹/₃ yard (.3m) of lining fabric

- Two contrasting-color spools of heavy twisted rayon thread, such as pearl rayon, for the decorative finishing; three spools of coordinating serger or all-purpose thread; coordinating all-purpose thread for the sewing machine

- Seam sealant

## Cutting directions:

- Cut two lining pieces following the pattern grid. (Fig. 8-29)

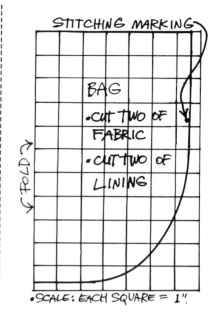

*Fig. 8-29 Cut the lining pieces now, then cut the fabric after you've done the serge-piecing.*

- The bag will be cut later from the pieced fabric.

### SERGER SETTINGS:

3-thread balanced stitch

**Stitch length:** Short

**Stitch width:** Narrow

**Needle:** Size 11/75

## How-tos:

Sew all seams using ¹/₄" (6mm) allowances, trimming the excess seam allowances.

1. Thread the rayon thread in both loopers and serger or all-purpose thread in the needle. Adjust your serger for a medium-length stitch. Begin testing the stitch by slowly turning the handwheel. You may need to tighten the upper and lower looper-thread tension slightly. Then gradually shorten the stitch length to perfect a satin stitch.

*Fig. 8-28 Rayon thread adds attractive detailing to the pieced fabric.*

2 Place two scraps of fabric wrong sides together and serge-seam, positioning the decorative serging on the right side of the fabric. Synthetic suede may be cut in any direction, so don't worry about grainlines. Continue piecing randomly until you have a section of pieced fabric measuring at least 24″ by 15″ (61cm by 38cm).

*WHEN CROSSING A SEAM OR SEAMS, BE SURE TO FOLD THE PREVIOUS SERGED ALLOWANCES SO THAT THE UPPER LOOPER STITCHING SHOWS ON THE TOP SIDE. (FIG. 8-30)*

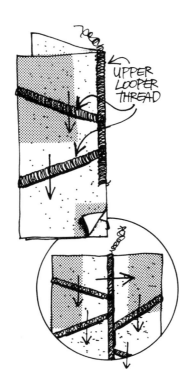

Fig. 8-30 *Be sure to fold the serged allowances on both layers so the upper looper stitching is up before serging a crossing seam.*

3 Cut two bag sections from the pieced rectangle, following the pattern grid in Fig. 8-29. Change to serger or all-purpose thread in the loopers and serge-finish around the outer edges of both sections, folding all the seam allowances so that the upper looper thread is on top.

4 With the right sides of one bag section and one lining section together, straight-stitch from the top edge down to the stitching marking dot on both sides, back-stitching to secure the ends. Repeat for the other bag and lining sections.

5 Turn one bag/lining section right side out and slip it into the other section with the right sides of the bag against each other and the right sides of the lining together. Matching the seamline on one side, straight-stitch along the seamline from the top of the bag, down 3″ (7.5cm), back-stitching to secure. Repeat for the opposite side of the bag. (Fig. 8-31)

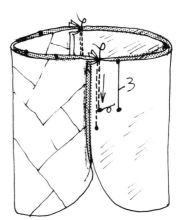

Fig. 8-31 *On both sides of the bag, straight-stitch the tops together along the first seamline.*

6 Folding the lining sections out of the way, place the right side edges of the bag together and straight-stitch around the curved bottom from marking to marking, back-stitching to secure the ends. Folding the bag out of the way, repeat for the lining. (Fig. 8-32) (This will leave a small section unstitched on both sides of the bag for the casing drawstring openings.)

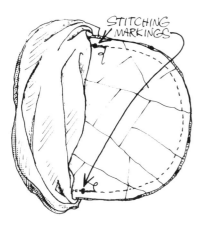

Fig. 8-32 *Straight-stitch around the bottom edges of the bag.*

7 Turn the bag right side out and serge-finish the upper edge through both the bag and lining. Lap the ends of the stitching ½"(1.3cm).

8 Turn the upper edge 2" (5cm) to the wrong side and tuck the serge-finishing thread-chain end under the hem casing. Top-stitch through the center of the serge-finishing. From the right side, top-stitch again ¾" (2cm) above the first row of stitching to form the casing.

9 To make the ties, fold the strips lengthwise, wrong sides together, matching the cut edges. Serge-finish the long lengthwise cut edge and the long folded edge. Then serge-finish the two short ends. Dab the corners with seam sealant and trim the excess thread when dry.

10 Thread both ties through the entire casing, beginning each one from the opening on opposite sides of the bag. Knot the ends of both ties and pull them to close the bag. Wear the bag over your shoulder, using the tie ends as shoulder straps. (Fig. 8-33)

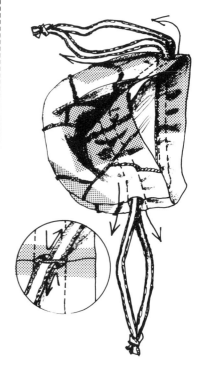

Fig. 8-33 *Thread both shoulder-strap ties completely through the casing from opposite directions, and knot the ends together.*

# Appendices

# Glossary

**ALL-PURPOSE THREAD**
All-purpose thread is usually cotton-covered polyester or 100% polyester wound parallel on conventional spools.

**BALANCED STITCH**
Serged stitching in which the upper- and lower-looper thread tensions are balanced so that the threads meet at the edge of the fabric, forming loops.

**BINDING**
A strip of fabric sewn or serged to an edge, then wrapped around it and secured to hide the seam and the raw edge.

**CHAIN OFF**
To run the serger for several inches past the fabric edge, forming a thread chain. This will usually hold the stitching intact until the end is serged over or secured by another method.

**CLEAR THE STITCH FINGER**
Remove the stitches that have formed over the serger's stitch finger. This is most often done by raising the presser foot and needle(s), pulling a little slack in the needle thread(s), and gently pulling the fabric or thread chain toward the back of the machine.

**DECORATIVE**
Any stitching on the outside of a garment or project that enhances design detail, usually using a decorative thread or trim.

**DECORATIVE THREAD**
Any contrasting thread other than all-purpose or serger thread, although even a contrasting color of these threads is technically considered decorative (see Chapter 8).

**DIFFERENTIAL-FEED SETTING**
The differential-feed mechanism, available on many sergers, can be adjusted to a high setting to gather fabric or help ease the edge so that it doesn't stretch as it is serged. The differential feed can also be adjusted to a low setting to hold the fabric taut or stretch it to lettuce an edge as it is serged.

**EASE-PLUS**
A manual option to the differential feed, accomplished by force-feeding fabric under the front of the presser foot and holding it from exiting out the back. (See Fig. 1-17)

**EDGE-STITCH**
A medium-length (10-12 stitches/inch) straight-stitch on a conventional sewing machine applied near the edge of the project. Edge-stitching is often used to join two serge-finished layers.

**FILLER CORD**
Crochet thread, pearl cotton, buttonhole twist, or other heavy thread that simulates piping when serged over with a short, satin-length stitch. Filler cord is also used for gathering after serging over it with a medium- to wide-width, balanced stitch.

**FLATLOCK**
A stitch type in which the needle thread is loose enough so that the serged stitches flatten out on top of the fabric, forming decorative loops when the fabric is pulled apart. The underside will show a ladder effect of evenly spaced double parallel stitches. Used both for seaming and decorative stitching on a folded edge.

**HEAVY THREAD**
Crochet thread, pearl cotton, or buttonhole twist used for serge-gathering or filler cord in serger piping.

**LONG STITCH**
A 4mm or 5mm serged stitch length.

**MACHINE-BASTE**
A long (6-8 stitches/inch) straight-stitch on a conventional sewing machine.

**MATCHING THREAD**
Thread the same color as (or that blends as well as possible with) the project fabric.

**MEDIUM-LENGTH STITCH**
A serged stitch length of about 3mm.

**MEDIUM-WIDTH STITCH**
A serged stitch width of about 3.5mm to 4.5mm.

**NARROW-WIDTH STITCH**
A 2mm to 3mm serged stitch width. Used to serge a narrow seam or edge.

**PIN-FIT THE PATTERN**
Pin the pattern pieces together on the seamlines and hold them up to your body to estimate the fit of the finished garment.

**READY-TO-WEAR**
Garments available for purchase through retail stores and mail-order outlets.

**ROLLED EDGE
(FINISH OR SEAM)**
Also called a narrow rolled edge or hem, this stitch is created by altering the tension so that the raw edge rolls to the underside. A short stitch length creates an attractive satin-stitch edge.

**SATIN-STITCH (SATIN-LENGTH)**
A stitch length short enough to allow the thread to cover the entire fabric over which it is serged. Appropriate for both a balanced stitch or a rolled edge.

**SECURE THE THREAD CHAIN**
Using one of several possible methods to keep the ends of serged stitching from raveling. Options include applying seam sealant and trimming the excess when dry, knotting the chain, feeding the chain under previous stitches using a hook or tapestry needle, or serging over previous stitches.

**SERGE-FINISH**
Most often a medium-length, medium-width, balanced 3- or 3/4-thread stitch used to finish the edge of one layer during the construction process.

**SERGE-GATHER**
Gathering an edge or fold by using of one of several serger techniques (see Chapter 4) before top-stitching or easing and serge-seaming it to another project section.

**SERGER THREAD**
Standard serger thread has the same fiber content but is lighter in weight than all-purpose thread and is crosswound on cones or tubes so that it feeds easily during higher-speed serger sewing.

**SERGE-SEAM**
Most often a wide, medium-length, balanced 3- or 3/4-thread stitch used to seam two layers together.

**SHORT STITCH**
A .75mm to 2mm serged stitch length.

**STITCH-IN-THE-DITCH**
Straight-stitching directly on top of a previous seamline to secure another layer positioned on the underside. Often used for nearly invisible stitching when applying a binding to an edge or securing elastic in a waistband.

**STITCH TYPES**
Distinctive stitches formed by a serger. (See Fig. 1-1)  Most serger models feature a combination of stitch types.

**STRAIGHT-STITCH**
A medium-length (10-12 stitches/inch) straight stitch on a conventional sewing machine.

**THREAD CHAIN**
The joined loops formed by serging on a properly threaded machine with no fabric.

**TOP-STITCH**
A conventional sewing-machine straight stitch (10-12 stitches/inch) used to attach one layer (often serge-finished) to another away from the project edge. Top-stitching also can be used as a decorative design detail.

**UNDER-STITCH**
To add a row of straight-stitching, usually close to the attached edge of a facing, that goes through both the facing and the seam allowance underneath and prevents the facing from rolling to the right side of the garment.

**WIDE STITCH**
A 5mm to 9mm serged stitch width.

**WOOLLY NYLON**
One of our favorite decorative threads that became popular with the advent of serger sewing. Now available in two weights, this crimped nylon thread fluffs out to fill any see-through spaces on a decorative edge.

**ZIGZAG STITCH**
A basic sewing-machine stitch forming a series of short, sharp angles.

# Serger Troubleshooting

Having trouble perfecting your serging? The problem is usually something you can remedy yourself without consulting a repair specialist. Quickly check the most likely possibilities:

*1* **Check the obvious.**
Is the machine plugged in and turned on? Are the covers closed? Is the presser foot lowered? Have you raised the thread guide pole to its highest position?

*2* **Look at the threading.**
One of the most common causes of stitching problems is the threading or rethreading. (See Threading Trouble-shooting in Chapter 4 in *ABC's of Serging*)

*3* **Examine the needle(s).**
Some repair specialists do this the very first thing.

- Are you using the exact needle type specified for your serger model? If not, you will likely have stitching problems or stitches won't form at all.

- Is the needle inserted correctly, all the way into the needle bar with the groove squarely in the front? If not, the stitches will be irregular or won't form at all. Tighten the set screw so the needle doesn't slip out of position.

- Is the needle burred, bent or dull? If so, you may get puckering, snagging, or skipped stitches. Even a new needle can be defective.

- Are you using the correct needle size? For heavy fabric or thread, you may need a larger needle. For delicate fabric and fine thread, a smaller needle will work best.

*4* **Is your tension adjustment correct?**
If your needle-thread tension is too tight, it can cause puckering or the thread will break. If the looper tensions aren't adjusted correctly, the stitching can be unbalanced, irregular, or puckered. When you change thread or fabric, always check the tension settings and readjust if necessary.

*5* **Are the knives dull or out of position?**
Test them by serging a piece of slippery, lightweight fabric. If the cutting is ragged and uneven, the softer blade should be replaced. Also check to see if the blades are properly engaged. Refer to your owner's manual for specific instructions or ask your dealer to demonstrate correct positioning if you are unsure.

*6* **Are the differential feed and presser-foot pressure adjusted correctly?**
Have you returned to a normal setting after serging a heavy, light, or stretchy fabric? Can you use either control to help prevent stretching or puckering (see Chapter 8 in *ABC's of Serging*)?

*7* **Have you used the correct serging techniques?**

- Are you feeding fabric through the machine correctly? Pulling the fabric through the machine as you serge can cause needle breakage, looper damage, and problems.

- On difficult fabrics, have you lifted the toe or the entire foot to insert the fabric under it to begin serging? This can prevent bunching of the thread and will start two layers feeding evenly.

- With slippery or heavy fabrics, are you holding the thread chain behind the presser foot to help start serging smoothly? If not, the stitches can bunch or jam under the foot.

- Are you using a high-quality, evenly twisted thread for best results? The weight should also be appropriate for the fabric. Some novelty threads cannot be used successfully on all brands and models of sergers, so always test first.

*8* **Are you using the right stitch length?**
A long stitch might cause puckering and a short stitch can cause stretching or jamming. Always test first before serging your garment or project.

*9* **Have you regularly cleaned and oiled the machine?**
See Care and Maintenance (page 138 in *ABC's of Serging*) for specific suggestions.

10 **Is your serger completely jammed?**
Removing the jam without damaging the fabric can be a delicate task. Use this procedure recommended by expert problem solver Sue Green-Baker:

- Remove the presser foot and disengage the knife (if possible).

- Cut the needle and upper looper threads close to the stitching. Then pull slack in the lower looper thread by tugging underneath the tension control.

- Rotate the handwheel back and forth to loosen the needle from the fabric. Raise the needle (if you can) and gently pull on the fabric until it is loosened. Pull the fabric toward the back of the machine, removing it from the stitch finger.

- If you can't raise the needle, loosen the needle screw and rotate the handwheel to bring the needle bar up.

- Gently remove the needle and loosen the fabric from the stitch finger.

**TO AVOID A JAM:**

- Never serge with the fabric edge to the right of the needle plate when the knives are disengaged. Because the extra fabric isn't trimmed, it can bunch in the stitches or jam in the loopers.

- Draw the thread chain toward the back of the machine before stitching.

- Keep the looper cover closed while stitching. Trimmings can get caught and tangled in the loopers.

- When serging with heavy thread in the looper(s), begin with a medium-length stitch and shorten gradually. The thread bulk can cause a jam if the stitch is too short.

- The fabric may be too thick to feed smoothly through the serger. If so, zigzag along the stitching line first to compress the layers.

# Mail-Order Resources

We recommend that every sewing enthusiast develop a special relationship with his or her local dealers and retailers for convenient advice and inspiration, plus the ease of coordinating purchases. However, when specialty items cannot be found locally, or when a home-sewer lives several miles from a sewing retailer, mail-order specialists are a worthwhile option.

## AUTHORS' NOTE:

In today's volatile business climate, any mail-order source list will change frequently. Please send your comments on any out-of-business notifications or unsatisfactory service to Tammy Young, 2269 Chestnut #269, San Francisco, CA 94123.

## Key to Abbreviations and Symbols:

SASE = Self-addressed, stamped (first-class) envelope

L-SASE = Large SASE (2-oz. first-class postage)

* = refundable with order

# = for information, brochure, or catalog

## Recommended Resources

**AARDVARK ADVENTURES**
P.O. Box 2449, Dept. TY, Livermore, CA 94551, 510/443-2687. Decorative serging thread, books, beads, buttons, bangles, plus an unusual assortment of related products. $2*#.

**CLOTILDE, INC.**
1909 S.W. First Ave., Ft. Lauderdale, FL 33315, 800/772-2891. Wide range of supplies, including special serger threads and notions, books, and videos. Free#.

**A GREAT NOTION SEWING SUPPLY LTD.**
13847 17A Ave., White Rock, B.C., Canada V4A 7H4, 604/538-2829. Hard-to-find sewing supplies. $1 U.S.*#.

**MADEIRA MARKETING LTD.**
600 E. 9th St., Michigan City, IN 46360, 219/873-1000. Popular decorative threads. SASE#.

**MILL END STORE**
Box 82098, Portland, OR 97282-0098, 503/786-1234. Broad selection of fabric, swatches on requested types of fabric, notions, trims, threads, and accessories. SASE#.

**NANCY'S NOTIONS, LTD.**
P.O. Box 683, Beaver Dam, WI 53916, 800/833-0690. Wide range of sewing and serging notions and accessories, threads and tools, interfacings and fabrics, books, and videos. Free#.

**NATIONAL THREAD & SUPPLY**
695 Red Oak Rd., Stockbridge, GA 30281, 800/847-1001, ext. 1688; in GA, 404/389-9115. Name-brand sewing supplies and notions. Free#.

**NEWARK DRESSMAKER SUPPLY**
Dept. TY2, P.O. Box 20730, Lehigh Valley, PA 18002-0730, 215/837-7500. Sewing notions, trims, buttons, and decorative threads. Free#.

**SEW-ART INTERNATIONAL**
P.O. Box 550, Bountiful, UT 84011. Decorative threads, notions, and accessories. $2*#.

**SEW/FIT CO.**
P.O. Box 397, Bedford Park, IL 60499, 800/547-4739. Sewing notions and accessories, cutting tables, cutting mats, special rulers, and T-squares. Free#.

**SEWING EMPORIUM**
1079 Third Ave. #B, Chula Vista, CA 91910, 619/420-3490. Hard-to-find sewing and serging notions and parts, sewing machine cabinets, custom-made machine accessories, and threads. $4.95* handbook and #.

**SEW GREAT**
P.O. Box 111446, Campbell, CA 95011. Sewing machine and serger needles and feet, plus books by Gale Grigg Hazen. Specify your brand and model when ordering machine accessories. L-SASE#.

**SOLO SLIDE FASTENERS, INC.**
P.O. Box 528, Stoughton, MA 02072, 800/343-9670. All types and lengths of zippers plus other selected notions. L-SASE#.

**SPEED STITCH**
3113-D Broadpoint Dr., Harbor Heights, FL 33983, 800/874-4115. Machine-art kits and supplies, including all-purpose, decorative, and specialty serging threads, books, and accessories. $3*#.

**TREADLEART**
25834 Narbonne Ave., Lomita, CA 90717, 800/327-4222, 301/534-5122. Books, sewing supplies, notions, decorative threads, and creative inspiration. $3*#.

**WEB OF THREAD**
3240 Lone Oak Rd., Suite 124, Paducah, KY 42003, 800/955-8185. Large assortment and color range of popular decorative threads. $2#.

**YLI CORPORATION**
482 N. Freedom Blvd., Provo, UT 84601, 800/854-1932 or 801/377-3900. Decorative, specialty, and all-purpose threads, yarns, and ribbons. $2.50#.

# Other Books By The Authors

**ABCS OF SERGING**
Chilton Book Company, 1991, $16.95. The complete guide to serger sewing basics, by Tammy Young and Lori Bottom.

**DISTINCTIVE SERGER GIFTS & CRAFTS**
Chilton Book Company, 1989, $14.95. The first book with one-of-a-kind serger projects using ingenious methods and upscale ideas, by Naomi Baker and Tammy Young.

**INNOVATIVE SERGING**
Chilton Book Company, 1989, $14.95. State-of-the-art techniques for overlock sewing, by Gail Brown and Tammy Young.

**INNOVATIVE SEWING**
Chilton Book Company, 1990, $14.95. The newest, best, and fastest sewing techniques, by Gail Brown and Tammy Young.

**KNOW YOUR** BABY LOCK
Chilton Book Company, 1990, $16.95. Ornamental serging techniques for all baby lock serger models, by Naomi Baker and Tammy Young.

**KNOW YOUR PFAFF**
HOBBYLOCK
Chilton Book Company, 1991, $17.95. Ornamental serging techniques for all Hobbylock serger models, by Naomi Baker and Tammy Young.

**KNOW YOUR SERGER**
Chilton Book Company1992, $16.95. Ornamental serging techniques and all-new projects for any serger brand, by Naomi Baker and Tammy Young.

**KNOW YOUR WHITE**
SUPERLOCK
Chilton Book Company, 1991, $16.95. Ornamental serging techniques for all Superlock serger models, by Naomi Baker and Tammy Young.

**SERGED GARMENTS IN MINUTES**
Chilton Book Company, 1992, $16.95. A complete guide to simple construction techniques, by Tammy Young and Naomi Baker.

**SEW SENSATIONAL GIFTS**
Chilton Book Company, 1993, $16.95. Unique projects for everyone with speedy serging tips throughout, by Naomi Baker and Tammy Young.

**SIMPLY SERGE ANY FABRIC**
Chilton Book Company, 1990, $14.95. Tips and techniques for successfully serging all types of fabric, by Naomi Baker and Tammy Young.

**TAMING DECORATIVE SERGING**
by Tammy Young, self-published 1991, $14.95. A step-by-step workbook teaching special techniques for glamorous decorative serging.

**TAMING YOUR FIRST SERGER**
by Lori Bottom, published by Tammy Young 1989, $14.95. A hands-on guide to basic serging skills in an easy-to-use workbook format.

# Index

# About The Authors

**Tammy Young** is known for creative ideas and techniques and for her precise, detailed instructions. A prolific writer, she has co-authored eleven previous Chilton books and continues to write for the *Sewing Update* and *Serger Update* newsletters, which she founded and managed until selling them in 1991.

She is also a sewing-industry consultant to Chilton and edits the *Sewing & Crafts Merchandiser* newsletter, which the company sends quarterly to independent retailers. And as a freelancer, she writes press releases for a San Francisco public relations firm.

Tammy grew up in Oregon and has a home economics degree from Oregon State University. She has an extensive background in the ready-to-wear fashion industry, having worked for major companies including Pendleton Woolen Mills, Jantzen, and Lily of France. She was also an extension agent and a high school home economics teacher.

Now living and working in San Francisco's Marina District, Tammy enjoys working on creative projects and dreaming up ideas to try in her "spare time." She travels frequently, most recently to exotic destinations such as Taiwan and Costa Rica, picking up trends and ideas for her writing.

**Naomi Baker** is a nationally recognized sewing and serging authority who writes regularly for major industry publications and has co-authored eight previous Chilton books with Tammy Young. She specializes in technique research and development and is well known for her dressmaking skills.

Reared in the Midwest, Naomi is a clothing and textiles graduate of Iowa State University and worked as an extension agent for five years. After working an additional ten years for Stretch & Sew, and experimenting with virtually every home serger on the market at that time, she decided to begin her own sewing consulting business.

In addition to her writing, Naomi is a consulting editor for the *Serger Update* newsletter, makes frequent guest appearances on national television shows, and teaches at special workshops and conventions across the country. She is also involved in numerous volunteer activities in her community.

Naomi lives and works in Springfield, Oregon, with her husband, family, and a house full of fabric, sewing supplies, and sergers. She feels fortunate to live in an area with lots of excellent sewing stores and a proportionate number of avid sewing and serging enthusiasts.